VISUAL STORYTELLING

VISUAL STORYTELLING

An Illustrated Reader

TODD JAMES PIERCE

California Polytechnic State University

RYAN G. VAN CLEAVE

Ringling College of Art and Design

NEW YORK   OXFORD
OXFORD UNIVERSITY PRESS

Oxford University Press is a department of the University of Oxford.
It furthers the University's objective of excellence in research,
scholarship, and education by publishing worldwide.

Oxford   New York
Auckland   Cape Town   Dar es Salaam   Hong Kong   Karachi
Kuala Lumpur   Madrid   Melbourne   Mexico City   Nairobi
New Delhi   Shanghai   Taipei   Toronto

With offices in
Argentina   Austria   Brazil   Chile   Czech Republic   France   Greece
Guatemala   Hungary   Italy   Japan   Poland   Portugal   Singapore
South Korea   Switzerland   Thailand   Turkey   Ukraine   Vietnam

Copyright © 2016 by Oxford University Press

For titles covered by Section 112 of the US Higher Education
Opportunity Act, please visit www.oup.com/us/he for the
latest information about pricing and alternate formats.

Published by Oxford University Press
198 Madison Avenue, New York, New York 10016
http://www.oup.com

Oxford is a registered trademark of Oxford University Press.

Library of Congress Cataloging-in-Publication Data
Visual storytelling : an illustrated reader / Todd Pierce, California Polytechnic
State University ; Ryan Van Cleave, Ringling College of Art and Design.
    pages cm
  Includes bibliographical references.
  ISBN 978-0-19-938004-6 (acid-free paper) -- ISBN 978-0-19-938005-3
(acid-free paper) 1. Comic books, strips, etc.--Themes, motives. 2. Graphic
novels--Themes, motives. 3. Storytelling in literature. 4. Narration (Rhetoric)
5. Visual literacy. 6. College readers. I. Pierce, Todd James, 1965- editor.
II. Van Cleave, Ryan G., 1972- editor.
  PN6714.V57 2015
  741.5'9--dc23
                                                          2015020334

Printing number: 9 8 7 6 5 4 3 2 1

Printed in the United States of America
on acid-free paper

"Today, comics is one of the very few forms of mass communication in which the individual voices still have a chance to be heard."

—SCOTT MCCLOUD

CONTENTS

As teachers of writing and literature, we daily witness the power of language in the classroom, in our writing, and in our public and private lives. Language preserves. Language provokes. Language questions. Language engages. Language reveals. Language enlarges. Language creates. It's both process and product. It's the mechanism that pushes open the walls of the world for us. It's one of the most powerful forces we have at our disposal.

These are just a few of the many reasons that we've made its study our lives' work.

Visual Storytelling, too, is a book that's indeed about language, but not just the verbal language of traditional classroom texts—it's a book about visual language as much as verbal language. What we've found in our combined four decades of teaching is that thoughtful, well-constructed "texts" in any sense of the word can provide the framework to have useful, impactful discussions on effective communication. And what better way to engage generations of visually inclined students than to showcase how visual + verbal texts—graphic narratives—are as rich and discussion-worthy as any canonical classroom text?

Edward Hopper, an American painter whose work slanted toward realism, once said, "If you could say it in words, there'd be no reason to paint." And it's this impulse that drives so many artists and illustrators to enter the world of graphic narratives.

What This Book Is Not

This book does not attempt to serve as an exhaustive history of the graphic novel. Nor is it a list of every worthwhile, talented writer and artist working in the field today. (If the history of comics interests you, check out our Further Readings appendix, which details some of the top creators and texts in the field.) It's also not designed to fully explore non-English texts such as those from the rich Franco-Belgian and Japanese traditions.

One of the challenges we faced with compiling a visual textbook for a literature or composition classroom is size and cost: we simply can't include everything. While we'd love to include the entire text of *Persepolis*, *Maus*, *Black Hole*, *Asterios Polyp*, and *American Widow*, we realized at the start that was impossible. But we did take care to choose works that were representative of a wide range of styles, narrative sensibilities, themes, and voices so that this textbook offers a good survey of contemporary comics, particularly as they relate to the common themes of literature and writing.

Additionally, this book is not an apology for the form. We understand that there are teachers who are so committed the traditional texts that nothing—not even significant advances in graphic forms—can shake them from the traditional, verbal canon. This book isn't for them. Instead, it's for teachers and students who are interested in the possibilities available to this rich, quickly expanding form. This form is uniquely suited to contemporary classrooms because it lends itself so well to discussions about art, history, literature, film, and composition.

The Term "Graphic Novel"

In some ways, "graphic novel" is a suitable term for a text that artfully combines written words and visuals. Will Eisner, a twentieth-century visual author and a giant in this field, popularized the term "graphic novel" to describe his book *A Contract with God*. He didn't want publishers to dismiss it by calling it a comic book. During his lifetime, "comic book" suggested something only for children, something that had few, if any, serious artistic aspirations.

But "graphic novel" is somewhat of a limiting term. What about those texts that aren't book length? Can we still call them novels? And what about when the subject matter isn't fiction?

Others have satisfied themselves with "comics," "comix," or "sequential art." The term we will primarily use throughout the book, however, is "graphic narrative." For us, that includes many forms, such as the graphic novel, the graphic memoir, the graphic essay, and the graphic short story. If you're a proponent of any other term for a text that combines words and images in a purposefully sequenced fashion, just understand that when we write "graphic novel" or "graphic narrative," we mean that, too.

How to Read Graphic Narratives

A graphic narrative might have a different physical look than a traditional verbal story by Charles Dickens or an essay by David Sedaris, but the many principles of reading verbal texts applies to visual texts as well. Start at the top left, then work your way to the bottom right. A single picture is referred to as a "panel." A row of panels is called a "tier." Most graphic narratives offer regular tiers of panels—like a line of text in a traditional book. Once you've finished the top tier, move down to the next row. Follow that same procedure all the way down the page, working panel by panel through it.

What if, in a single panel, you find dialogue in multiple balloons or more than one caption? Follow the same basic procedure: read top left to right, then repeat the process all the way down the panel.

The white space between panels is called a "gutter." It borders the image and separates one panel from the next. If you ever see the illustrations continue beyond the borders, that's meaningful, as it often suggest that one element from the first panel "bleeds" into the next. Pay attention to it.

If you ever notice that the text says one thing yet the images work in contrast to it, that too is quite likely meaningful and worthy of serious consideration. Just as in real life, a person's words don't always match his or her actions. In a graphic text, use both verbal and visual cues to understand characterization.

It's also useful to pay attention to how words are delivered visually. Fonts, balloon shapes, and typography matter in a graphic text.

In the following example, the words that appear in the box are often called the "caption." They are *usually* the narrative voice of the story—though remember: sometimes the main character can also be the narrator of his or her story. Consider these words like you would a paragraph of exposition in a novel or a section of voice-over in film.

(Note: a few artists complicate the issue by using this technique for thoughts or even dialogue. So as with any reading assignment, pay attention to any unique strategies an author may use in a particular text.)

A Few Tips on Reading Graphic Narratives

When you encounter a graphic narrative—in these pages or elsewhere—read it slowly and then reread. Many graphic narratives have so little text on the page that it's easy to get swept up in the story and sprint through it. There are three reasons to slow down, however. (1) If there's only a little text, the words that are included are likely quite important. (2) Characters in graphic texts communicate through gesture and facial expression, not just words. Study each panel to understand the nonverbal communication implicit in each image. (3) Beyond the characters themselves, other visual elements often inform and texture the story. These elements include artistic style, the color palette, drawing scale, the framing of each image, and so on. Don't ignore those elements. In some texts, they can be more meaningful than the actual words.

After an initial read, review the text for complexities you might have missed the first time. Ask questions to deepen your understanding as you view the text through multiple lenses.

- What's the main story? (Whose story is it? And why does this story matter to the main character?)
- How does the author create tone? Mood? Is it mostly through words, plot, characterization, or artistic style?
- What is the connection between the mood of the plot and the mood of the visual elements?
- Does this narrative rely on knowledge of other cultural elements to more fully understand it? For example, does this narrative offer a parody of a popular film? Is this narrative a retelling of a traditional, verbal short story? Does this narrative rely on a reader's understanding of a historical event, religious narrative, or political controversy?
- Is the form and/or content of the work meaningfully informed by one or more aspects of the author's identity—such as gender, sexual orientation, ethnicity, religious views, and so on? How so?
- Does this narrative offer or support a compelling worldview or political position? For example, does it offer an argument against extremism? Or does this narrative critique Western commercialism? Does it have anything to say about the nature of art?
- What type of symbols (images repeated with meaning) do you find in the text? How do they add to or texture the meaning found in the narrative?

Overall, with graphic narratives, you should have the same high level of expectations that you would for traditional canonical literature. The critical skills you use in carefully reading a poem like Wilfred Owen's "Dulce et Decorum Est" or a short story like Tim O'Brien's "The Things They Carried" will serve you well in encountering, understanding, and appreciating any other text.

Going Forward

Graphic narratives are far more than just a tier of panels with some artwork and words. Many of the best graphic writers and artists are consciously drawing upon the literary traditions of the novel, the essay, the dramatic play, the poem, and art-house cinema. They see their work as an expansion of previous literary traditions, a field that combines the communication elements of verbal literature with those of art. Will graphic narratives ever replace verbal texts? We seriously doubt it. But we do believe that they now offer a compelling new genre, with the best visual work able to stand toe-to-toe with the best verbal work produced today.

And beyond their artistic and narrative merit, as we've assembled this textbook, we've found many reasons to believe that graphic narratives will soon be a regular part of the textual landscape at most every college.

1) Studies show that graphic texts help people retain information better than traditional written texts. (Check out "Graphic Presentation: An Empirical Examination of the Graphic Novel Approach to Communicate Business Concepts," a study by Jeremy Short of the University of Oklahoma. There's also a TedxOU talk by Short titled "Graphic Textbooks: A Graphic Approach to Higher Education" that's well worth watching.)

2) Reading graphic novels is a participatory act. Decoding meaning in a graphic text takes as much patience and skill as reading a verbal text.

3) Graphic texts can serve as a unique way to emphasize and explore aspects of narrative, history, critical theory, and personal experience, by combining the traditions of verbal literature with the traditions of world art, photography, and printmaking.

4) There's already a big audience for them. Ask any librarian—they have trouble keeping graphic narratives of all types on the shelves.

5) More and more scholars are taking up the study of graphic narratives. As Laura Jiménez, who did her PhD work in graphic narratives and now hosts a website to promote their educational use (booktoss.wordpress.com), explains: "If we can teach educators how to read like experts, they may be more likely to use books that are complex, interesting, and rich."

Closing

For the past three years, we've worked through thousands of graphic texts to find the stories, essays, and other narratives now assembled in this textbook. We think that you, the reader, are in for a treat, as you discover the richness of this world. In short, we love graphic narratives, and we hope that after reading the selections in this book, you will too. Moreover, we hope that you will find these graphic narratives an interesting starting point for reflection, discussion, and various response projects.

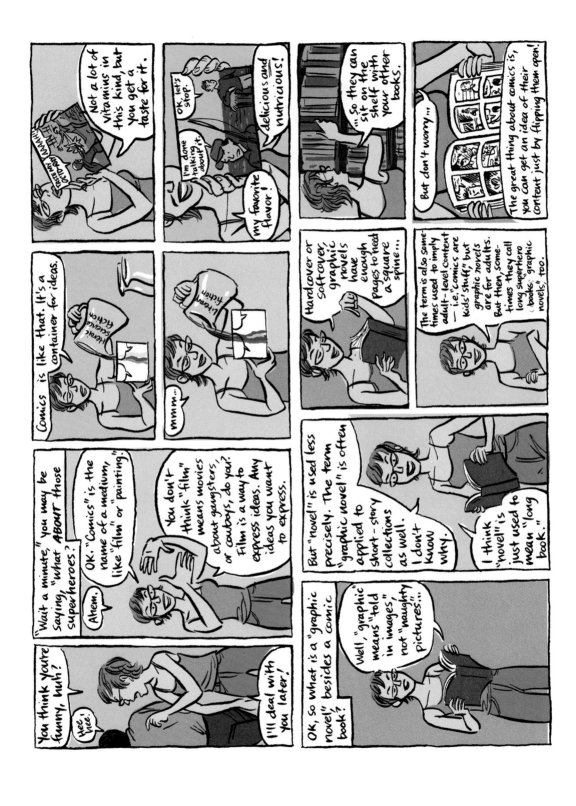

VISUAL STORYTELLING

Identity

Most everyone knows the common definition of "identity." To identify a person means to define a person with surety. When you travel to a foreign country, you identify yourself by producing your passport—that is, you define your name, age, and nationality with authority. When a police detective says, "I have determined the identity of the thief," she means that she has revealed the name of the thief with confidence. Literature, however, uses the term "identity" in a different way. In a literature class, the term means one of two things: (1) the way in which a character is marked by being a member of a social group (such as how the character Kelly has been marked by being a woman) and/or (2) a distinguishing value or experience that has played a significant role in shaping the personality of a character (such as how the character Steven allowed his social identity to be shaped by his sexual orientation). Identity, in loose terms, is the relationship between the social groups a character belongs to (nationality, gender, religious communities, etc.) and the formation of a public and private personality.

To better define the relationship between social groups and personality, let's use you, the reader, as an example of someone who possesses a complex *identity*. All people belong to multiple social groups: ethnic communities, educational institutions, gender groups, and so on. Reflect on the following questions, noting the ways that the values and markings of social groups in part shaped your present identity.

1) How has your parents' religious community—or lack of religious community—influenced the way you view the world?
2) How has your sexual orientation shaped the ways you present yourself to others and how you establish relationship goals for the future?
3) How has your gender—particularly popular conceptions about masculinity and femininity—framed how you solicit attention from people and, therefore, create a public image?
4) How does your race—or your understanding of race—allow you to act within or without systems of social privilege?

Just like you, characters in contemporary literature belong to multiple social groups—from gender to ethnicity and beyond. Migrant literature often examines how a character is influenced by multiple national or ethnic cultures. The literature of gender often examines the identity of women and men as it relates to social conceptions of masculine and feminine roles. The concerns of identity—the mysterious ways in which personality is affected and developed by a person's inclusion in various social groups—is also explored in the work of graphic narratives. Or, more simply put, it is explored in comics.

Comics explore the concerns of identity through both language and illustration. The way a character is marked may be demonstrated by dialogue, action, *or* visual presentation. For a visual culture such as ours, comics are able to explore identity in new ways—through facial expression, bodily gesture, and even a graphic style selected by the artist.

In the following pages, comic artists will work with some core aspects of identity. In her graphic travelogue, Sarah Glidden—born in America and raised in a Jewish family—travels to Israel and struggles to connect her present beliefs with nationalistic propaganda promoted in her ancestral country. In his graphic essay, Jeremy Sorese explores how his experience as a gay man with divorced parents has influenced his own understanding of and expectations for romantic love. In her autobiographical comic *Persepolis*, Marjane Satrapi explores how the religious customs and beliefs of Islam combined with the progressive values of her family formed her young worldview and her expectations for the future.

The concept of identity isn't, of course, limited to this section. This textbook is filled with graphic narratives that explore issues of identity—such as "La Brea Woman" by Martin Cendreda and "Cecil and Jordan in New York" by Gabrielle Bell, both of them in later sections. But here, with our introductory offerings, we'd like to introduce not only the movements of contemporary comics but how—with these fine examples—they relate to and develop the concerns of traditional literature, such as those that define the complexities of identity.

JEREMY SORESE

"Love Me Forever! Oh! Oh! Oh!"

Jeremy Sorese was born in Berlin and raised in suburban Virginia. He earned a BFA in sequential art at the Savannah College of Art and Design. Following two years working odd jobs in Chicago, he became a resident of La Maison des Auteurs in Angoulême, France, a residency program focused on comics and visual storytelling. Presently he resides in Brooklyn, New York. His first graphic novel, *Curveball* was published by Nobrow Press in 2015.

SORESE

LOVE ME FOREVER! Oh! Oh! Oh!
Recently, my divorced parents remarried
My Mom said "I DO" on a Sunset beach on the coast of Cape Cod
My Dad did the same at sunrise in Ocean City, months later

When I see photos of newly married gay couples, I can't help but see an eager groom and his best man, waiting for a tardy bride.

The ritual of marriage is too tied to gender specific symbols to encapsulate anything but the most traditional of matrimonial blisses.

AFTER YOU.

IN A GAY MARRIAGE...

WHO IS WALKED DOWN THE AISLE?

NOT AFTER LABOR DAY!

WHO WEARS WHITE?

I DO! I DO!

WHOSE PARENTS PAY FOR THE REHEARSAL DINNER?

For an older homosexual generation, the need for "pride", to stand up for what has been denied feels more important than it ever has for me.

I'd go as far to say that pride parades are as much public vows of love and devotion as the weddings of my parents. Each, in their ritual and costuming try to prove that what their heart feels is made legitimate in the eyes of an insensitive world.

✱ PAULA ABDUL, "STRAIGHT UP"

I think my lack of enthusiasm for gay marriage is more likely due to the fact that I'm only twenty-three. Sure a boyfriend would be phenomenal

(to cook breakfast for, to get lost in their eyes, wearing matching sweaters with)

At my dad's wedding, at the same hotel, a friend from highschool was also getting married!

JENNIFER?
JESSICA?
JAMIE?
JULIE?

When I hear of friends getting engaged at my age, I always feel apprehensive.
(AND HAPPY! Sorry friends)

The equal right to get married ensures nothing more than having one less hurdle in my life

After so many rough years, seeing my parents so happy with someone was phenomenal

When my mom made eye contact with anyone, she instantly burst into tears.

My dad, beaming, ear to ear, the whole day through.

Its strange to think of my parents going through the same romantic struggles I deal with. Strange but reassuring.

Marriage should be, in all its importance, a glue that unites two people. A solid, tangible bond...

like a button held tight within its hole.

But, obviously it isn't like that.

Upholding the sanctity of marriage is not about love but the traditions.

And I'm not destroying the institution of marriage on my wedding day any more than my parents, with their silver goblets and sand rituals, are.

(well... when that day happens)

I'm learning it takes a lifetime of missteps for that single day of grace.

J. Sorese '11   for my family

Introductory Questions

As "Love Me Forever! Oh! Oh! Oh!" is the first selection in our textbook, we've added a few additional questions to help you reflect on the difference between traditional texts and graphic texts.

(1) In your reading experience, do you gravitate first to the illustration or the text?

(2) What descriptive or narrative elements are included only in the illustrations and not in the text? How do these affect your reading?

(3) In your opinion, how is the experience of reading a graphic text similar to or different from reading a traditional text? What is gained from the inclusion of graphic elements in an essay or story? What is lost by replacing some language with illustration?

(4) When reading traditional text, students often examine the language closely to better understand the meaning. What additional skills are needed to analyze a visual text?

(5) Outside of academic assignments, do you find that most texts are (a) primarily image-based, (b) primarily language-based, or (c) a combination of image and language?

Analyze

(1) While this piece focuses on a single character and that character's worldview, in many ways it reads more like an essay than a story. Why is this essay-like quality an effective way to explore this particular topic? What specific advantages does an essay offer over a more traditional narrative?

(2) The essay suggests that participants in Western weddings (with the white gowns and tuxedos) and gay pride parades allow participants to partake in roles through costuming. What do the costumes of the Western wedding suggest about the roles the "husband" and "wife" adopt for their wedding day? What do the costumes of the gay pride parade suggest about the role parade participants adopt for the day?

(3) The presentation of the father's second wedding and the mother's second wedding are presented with different color palettes. What do the different color schemes suggest about how the author views his father and mother?

(4) Near the conclusion of the piece, the author writes, "Walking down an aisle will always be easier than a lifetime of love and trust in another human." What do you make of this statement? Hopeful? Cynical? Ironical? Something else? Do you agree with its sentiment? Why or why not?

Explore

(1) The author claims that his values differ from those of the previous generation: "For an older homosexual generation, the need for 'pride,' to stand up for what has been denied, feels more important than it ever has for me." Identify and

explore one value pertaining to romantic relationships that has changed from your parents' generation to your own—such as dating, sexual frankness, gender roles within romance, sense of sentimentality, openness of sexual identities, and so on. How has this change altered the nature of romance for your generation?

(2) The title of this work comes from a 1988 hit song by Paula Abdul. Why did the author choose this reference as the title? And why did he quote the song lyrics again in the middle of the piece, even going so far as to cite this usage at the bottom of the page? Use the Internet to find the complete lyrics for this song and see whether that offers any insight on the author's choices here. What contemporary song do you feel accurately expresses your own feelings on love?

(3) The author feels "happy" and "apprehensive" when his friends announce their engagements. His contradictory feelings are likely tied to his family experiences with having divorced parents who have gone on to marry other people. Define your feelings about marriage in general. Do you believe that, like the author, your feelings are closely linked to your own family experiences?

(4) In a small group, make a list of fifteen attitudes and experiences that best define romance for your generation. Also, list the ten films, books, TV shows, and songs that have most influenced your generation's understanding of romantic love and dating relationships?

MARJANE SATRAPI

Persepolis: The Story of a Childhood

Born in 1969 in Rasht, Iran, Marjane Satrapi grew up in Tehran in a middle-class family; she is also related to the Qajar Dynasty through her grandfather. Her parents were worried their strong-willed child would run afoul of the government, so they sent her to Vienna, Austria, to study at the Lycée Français de Vienne. In her graphic memoir *Persepolis*, she explains how after nearly dying of pneumonia, she returned to Tehran and obtained a master's degree in visual communication from Islamic Azad University. *Persepolis* has become a bestseller and was named a *New York Times* Notable Book and a *Time* magazine "Best Comix of the Year." Originally published in French, it has since been translated into forty languages. In addition to books for adults, Satrapi has written children's books, including *Monsters Are Afraid of the Moon*. The multitalented Satrapi has also worked as a film scriptwriter and/or director on *Persepolis*, *Chicken with Plums*, *The Gang of the Jotas*, and *Voices*.

THE VEIL

This is me when I was 10 years old. This was in 1980.

And this is a class photo. I'm sitting on the far left so you don't see me. From left to right: Golnaz, Mahshid, Narine, Minna.

In 1979 a revolution took place. It was later called "The Islamic Revolution".

Then came 1980: the year it became obligatory to wear the veil at school.

WEAR THIS!

We didn't really like to wear the veil, especially since we didn't understand why we had to.

IT'S TOO HOT OUT!

EXECUTION IN THE NAME OF FREEDOM.

OOH! I'M THE MONSTER OF DARKNESS.

GIVE ME MY VEIL BACK!

YOU'LL HAVE TO LICK MY FEET!

GIDDYAP!

AND ALSO BECAUSE THE YEAR BEFORE, IN 1979, WE WERE IN A FRENCH NON-RELIGIOUS SCHOOL.

WHERE BOYS AND GIRLS WERE TOGETHER.

AND THEN SUDDENLY IN 1980...

ALL BILINGUAL SCHOOLS MUST BE CLOSED DOWN.

THEY ARE SYMBOLS OF CAPITALISM.

BRAVO!

WHAT WISDOM!

OF DECADENCE.

THIS IS CALLED A "CULTURAL REVOLUTION."

WE FOUND OURSELVES VEILED AND SEPARATED FROM OUR FRIENDS.

AND THAT WAS THAT...

EVERYWHERE IN THE STREETS THERE WERE DEMONSTRATIONS FOR AND AGAINST THE VEIL.

AT ONE OF THE DEMONSTRATIONS, A GERMAN JOURNALIST TOOK A PHOTO OF MY MOTHER.

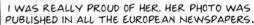

I WAS REALLY PROUD OF HER. HER PHOTO WAS PUBLISHED IN ALL THE EUROPEAN NEWSPAPERS.

AND EVEN IN ONE MAGAZINE IN IRAN. MY MOTHER WAS REALLY SCARED.

HAVE YOU SEEN THIS?

DON'T WORRY, DARLING.

SHE DYED HER HAIR,

AND WORE DARK GLASSES FOR A LONG TIME.

I REALLY DIDN'T KNOW WHAT TO THINK ABOUT THE VEIL. DEEP DOWN I WAS VERY RELIGIOUS BUT AS A FAMILY WE WERE VERY MODERN AND AVANT-GARDE.

I WAS BORN WITH RELIGION.

AT THE AGE OF SIX I WAS ALREADY SURE I WAS THE LAST PROPHET. THIS WAS A FEW YEARS BEFORE THE REVOLUTION.

O' Celestial light!

BEFORE ME THERE HAD BEEN A FEW OTHERS.

A WOMAN?

I AM THE LAST PROPHET.

I WANTED TO BE A PROPHET...

BECAUSE OUR MAID DID NOT EAT WITH US.

BECAUSE MY FATHER HAD A CADILLAC.

AND, ABOVE ALL, BECAUSE MY GRANDMOTHER'S KNEES ALWAYS ACHED.

COME HERE MARJI! HELP ME TO STAND UP.

DON'T WORRY. SOON YOU WON'T HAVE ANY MORE PAIN. YOU'LL SEE.

LIKE ALL MY PREDECESSORS I HAD MY HOLY BOOK.

THE FIRST THREE RULES CAME FROM ZARATHUSTRA. HE WAS THE FIRST PROPHET IN MY COUNTRY BEFORE THE ARAB INVASION.

YOU MUST BASE EVERYTHING ON THESE THREE RULES: BEHAVE WELL, SPEAK WELL, ACT WELL.

I ALSO WANTED US TO CELEBRATE THE TRADITIONAL ZARATHUSTRIAN HOLIDAYS. LIKE THE FIRE CEREMONY,

BEFORE THE PERSIAN NEW YEAR, NOROUZ, ON MARCH 21ST, THE FIRST DAY OF SPRING.

ONLY MY GRANDMOTHER KNEW ABOUT MY BOOK.

RULE NUMBER SIX: EVERY-BODY SHOULD HAVE A CAR.

RULE NUMBER SEVEN: ALL MAIDS SHOULD EAT AT THE TABLE WITH THE OTHERS.

RULE NUMBER EIGHT: NO OLD PERSON SHOULD HAVE TO SUFFER.

IN THAT CASE, I'LL BE YOUR FIRST DISCIPLE.

REALLY?

BUT TELL ME HOW YOU'LL ARRANGE FOR OLD PEOPLE NOT TO SUFFER?

IT WILL SIMPLY BE FORBIDDEN.

EVERY NIGHT I HAD A BIG DISCUSSION WITH GOD.

GOD, GIVE ME SOME MORE TIME. I AM NOT QUITE READY YET.

YES YOU ARE, CELESTIAL LIGHT, YOU ARE MY CHOICE, MY LAST AND MY BEST CHOICE.

EXCEPT FOR MY GRANDMOTHER I WAS OBVIOUSLY THE ONLY ONE WHO BELIEVED IN MYSELF.

WHAT DO YOU WANT TO BE WHEN YOU GROW UP?

vion
A - a

I'LL BE A PROPHET.

HAHA! HAHA! HAHA!

SHE'S CRAZY.

MY PARENTS WERE CALLED IN BY THE TEACHER.

YOUR CHILD IS DISTURBED. SHE WANTS TO BECOME A PROPHET.

WHAT ABOUT IT?

DOESN'T THIS WORRY YOU?

NO! NOT AT ALL!

?

Identity

NONETHELESS, MY PARENTS WERE PUZZLED.

SO TELL ME, MY CHILD, WHAT DO YOU WANT TO BE WHEN YOU GROW UP?

A PROPHET.

I WANT TO BE A DOCTOR.

THAT'S FINE MY LOVE. THAT'S FINE.

I FELT GUILTY TOWARDS GOD.

YOU WANT TO BE A DOCTOR? I THOUGHT THAT...

NO, NO, I WILL BE A PROPHET BUT THEY MUSTN'T KNOW.

I WANTED TO BE JUSTICE, LOVE AND THE WRATH OF GOD ALL IN ONE.

THE BICYCLE

MY FAITH WAS NOT UNSHAKABLE.

THE YEAR OF THE REVOLUTION I HAD TO TAKE ACTION. SO I PUT MY PROPHETIC DESTINY ASIDE FOR A WHILE.

TODAY MY NAME IS CHE GUEVARA.

I AM FIDEL.

AND I WANT TO BE TROTSKY.

WE DEMONSTRATED IN THE GARDEN OF OUR HOUSE.

DOWN WITH THE KING!

DOWN WITH THE KING!

THE REVOLUTION IS LIKE A BICYCLE. WHEN THE WHEELS DON'T TURN, IT FALLS.

WELL SPOKEN!

AND SO WENT THE REVOLUTION IN MY COUNTRY.

"AFTER A LONG SLEEP OF 2500 YEARS, THE REVOLUTION HAS FINALLY AWAKENED THE PEOPLE."

"2500 YEARS OF TYRANNY AND SUBMISSION" AS MY FATHER SAID.

FIRST OUR OWN EMPERORS.

THEN THE ARAB INVASION FROM THE WEST.

FOLLOWED BY THE MONGOLIAN INVASION FROM THE EAST.

AND FINALLY MODERN IMPERIALISM.

TO ENLIGHTEN ME THEY BOUGHT BOOKS.

I KNEW EVERYTHING ABOUT THE CHILDREN OF PALESTINE.

ABOUT FIDEL CASTRO.

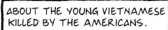

ABOUT THE YOUNG VIETNAMESE KILLED BY THE AMERICANS.

ABOUT THE REVOLUTIONARIES OF MY COUNTRY...

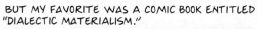

BUT MY FAVORITE WAS A COMIC BOOK ENTITLED "DIALECTIC MATERIALISM."

IN MY BOOK YOU COULD SEE MARX AND DESCARTES.

THE MATERIAL WORLD DOESN'T EXIST, IT'S ONLY A REFLECTION OF OUR OWN IMAGINATION.

SAYS YOU!

Identity

THE FIREMEN DIDN'T ARRIVE UNTIL FORTY MINUTES LATER.

THE BBC SAID THERE WERE 400 VICTIMS. THE SHAH SAID THAT A GROUP OF RELIGIOUS FANATICS PERPETRATED THE MASSACRE. BUT THE PEOPLE KNEW THAT IT WAS THE SHAH'S FAULT !!!

Analyze

(1) Why does Marjane Satrapi let only her grandmother know about the holy book she's writing? In what way is the grandmother truly her "first disciple"?

(2) How important is it that despite reading so many books about dissidents and revolutionaries, it was a comic book that truly inspired her? And how relevant is it that it's a comic book called Dialectic Materialism? What other "big ideas" have been explored in graphic form? What advantage does the graphic form allow for tackling abstract concepts and big ideas like these?

(3) How literally do you think you're supposed to take her conversations with God? What do you make of the observation that "it was funny to see how much [Karl] Marx and God looked like each other. Though Marx's hair was a bit curlier"? What other humorous moments do you find in this excerpt?

(4) What connection do you see between revolution and religion? Is there any way to reconcile the two? Why or why not? Which of these two forces do you see as more powerful in the world today? Explain.

Explore

(1) Whether you've read *Persepolis* beyond this excerpt or not, imagine what should come next after the final panel. Sketch your thoughts, and include dialogue too. Consider sharing your response with a friend and discussing the similarities and differences in your ideas of where the story seems to be going.

(2) Satrapi's parents are deeply committed Marxists. Find out more about Karl Marx and his basic belief system that they're following. How do you see those beliefs playing out in Satrapi's parents' lives? Her own?

(3) *Persepolis* has a lot in common with Art Spiegelman's Pulitzer Prize–winning graphic novel *Maus*, beyond the black-and-white notepad-style illustrations. Read both texts, and then consider how each author handles the following ideological concerns:
- Isolation
- Law
- Family
- Violence
- Belief systems

(4) *Persepolis* was made into a film. View it, and then compare it to your reading of the excerpt in this textbook, or even the entire graphic novel. Which is more effective? Why? What scenes are handled differently in the movie version?

SARAH GLIDDEN

"How to Understand Israel"

In "How to Understand Israel," Sarah Glidden explores her connection to the Middle East in a graphic narrative that is part diary, part historical essay, and part political argument. She has a BFA from Boston University, and her work contributes to a new movement among graphic artist that combines traditional journalism with graphic elements. Her book *How to Understand Israel in 60 Days or Less* was published in 2011 by DC Vertigo. Presently she is working on a second book of journalistic illustration documenting her time accompanying reporters stationed in Turkey, Lebanon, Iraq, and Kurdistan.

GLIDDEN

WHILE EVERYONE ELSE IS FINISHING UP WITH THEIR LUNCH, I GO FOR A LITTLE WALK TO EXPLORE KATZRIN. WHAT A STRANGE PLACE.

WHAT DOES IT MEAN TO LIVE IN "DISPUTED TERRITORY"?

DO YOU JUST IGNORE THE CONTROVERSY AND TRY TO LIVE YOUR LIFE LIKE NORMAL?

OR DOES IT DEFINE YOU?

EITHER WAY, THIS ISN'T THE WARMEST OF PLACES WHEN IT COMES TO URBAN PLANNING.

GIFTS FROM ISRAEL

THE COLDNESS COULD BE DELIBERATE. IN THE EVENT THAT THEY HAVE TO RETURN THIS LAND TO SYRIA, WOULD ANYONE REALLY MISS IT?

HELLO!

OH! HELLO!

HELLO!

Identity

THE LIGHTS DIM AND THREE PROJECTORS LIGHT UP AN IMAX-STYLE SCREEN WITH A SWEEPING AERIAL SHOT OF THE GOLAN HEIGHTS IN FULL BLOOM.

THE GOLAN HEIGHTS...SINCE ISRAEL WON THIS LAND IN THE SIX-DAY WAR IT HAS BEEN AN IMPORTANT PART OF THIS NATION'S LIFEBLOOD.

IT SUPPLIES ALMOST A THIRD OF ISRAEL'S WATER SUPPLY AND IS A CENTER OF AGRICULTURE AND HERDING.

NOT TO MENTION RECREATION!

FROM THE SNOWY PEAK OF MOUNT HERMON...

...TO THE WORLD-FAMOUS VALLEY WINERIES...

CLINK!

THE GOLAN HEIGHTS' UNIQUE TERRAIN SUPPORTS ITS OWN POPULATION OF 30,000 AS WELL AS THE THOUSANDS OF VISITORS WHO COME TO SEE ITS MAJESTY.

MOST IMPORTANT, ITS GEOGRAPHIC POSITION MAKES IT INDISPENSABLE TO THE NATION'S SECURITY. BEFORE THE WAR, SYRIA SENT ROCKET ATTACKS INTO ISRAELI VILLAGES BELOW.

SYRIA

ROCKETS

ISRAEL

AND NOW...SYRIA WANTS IT BACK. ISRAEL HAS TRIED TO COMPROMISE WITH THE SYRIAN GOVERNMENT...

SYRIA

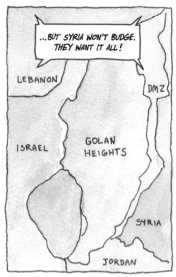

...BUT SYRIA WON'T BUDGE. THEY WANT IT ALL!

LEBANON

DMZ

ISRAEL

GOLAN HEIGHTS

SYRIA

JORDAN

EVERY BLADE OF GRASS, EVERY LAST PEBBLE, EVERY DROP OF WATER.

WOAH, SARAH...

YEAH. WOAH.

"MY FAMILY HAS LIVED HERE FOR FOUR GENERATIONS. THIS IS OUR HOME. TO GIVE IT UP WOULD BE TO GIVE UP MY HEART."

למסור את חגולן זה למסור את לבי

HMPH. THAT'S A TOTAL LIE. FOR HER FAMILY TO HAVE BEEN THERE FOR FOUR GENERATIONS THEY WOULD HAVE HAD TO BE THERE FOR WAY MORE THAN THE FORTY YEARS ISRAEL HAD CONTROL OVER THE TERRITORY!

"WITHDRAWAL FROM THE GOLAN HEIGHTS IS UNTHINKABLE, EVEN IN TIMES OF PEACE. IT WOULD MEAN ABANDONING ISRAEL'S SECURITY."

זה מסכן את ביטחוני ישראל

A GHOSTLY YITZHAK RABIN FLOATS OVER THE LANDSCAPE.

"LET ALL OF US FULFILL OUR OBLIGATIONS TO THE GOLAN HEIGHTS. AND TO YOU RESIDENTS THERE WHO MADE IT WHAT IT IS, YOU HAVE ALL MY RESPECT."

אני מכבד אותך

WHO CAN ARGUE WITH AN ASSASSINATED NOBEL PRIZE WINNER?

WHO CAN DISAGREE?

UM...

I KNEW IT! THIS WHOLE TRIP IS GOING TO BE A REGIONAL PROPAGANDA TOUR!

YOU GUYS THOUGHT IT WAS PROPAGANDA?

YOU DIDN'T?

I DUNNO...I THOUGHT IT WAS PRETTY COOL. I LIKE LEARNING MORE ABOUT THE AREA.

I THINK IT STARTED OUT OKAY...BUT THEN IT GOT WEIRD. IT WASN'T REALLY BALANCED LIKE A NEWS REPORT.

IT WASN'T BALANCED AT ALL!

WELL, LOOK AT IT A DIFFERENT WAY: UNTIL 1967 THE GOLAN HEIGHTS WAS JUST A LAUNCH PAD SO THEY COULD ATTACK KIBBUTZIM. THAT PART WAS TRUE AT LEAST.

WE HAVE MOVED INTO A ROOM NEXT TO THE THEATER WITH A GIGANTIC MODEL OF THE GOLAN HEIGHTS.

...AND DON'T GET ME WRONG, I FEEL FOR THESE PEOPLE! IT'S NOT THE SYRIAN VILLAGERS' FAULT THAT THEIR GOVERNMENT GOT SO AGGRESSIVE.

HEY, GIL? UM...

YES?

WELL...DON'T YOU THINK THAT WAS A LITTLE HEAVY ON THE PROPAGANDA?

VERY. AND I PROMISE YOU WE'LL ADDRESS THAT ISSUE. BUT NOT HERE, OKAY? ON THE BUS.

OKAY.

NOW IF YOU WOULD TURN YOUR ATTENTION TO THIS MODEL, WE CAN SEE WHY THE GOLAN HEIGHTS HAS BEEN IN THE MIDDLE OF THIS ARGUMENT.

IN THE NINETEEN YEARS PRIOR TO THE SIX DAY-WAR, THERE WAS A LOT OF HARASSMENT FROM THE SYRIAN ARMY DOWN TO THE ISRAELI AREAS BELOW, AND THAT'S WHY ISRAEL DECIDED TO CAPTURE IT.

ACTUALLY, THE SIX DAY WAR WAS THREE DIFFERENT CAMPAIGNS. TWO DAYS AGAINST THE EGYPTIANS, TWO AGAINST THE JORDANIANS, AND THE LAST TWO AGAINST THE SYRIANS.

THIS RIDGE GOES ALL THE WAY FROM LEBANON TO ETHIOPIA, AND MOST OF THE BATTLES ON THE SYRIAN FRONT WERE FOUGHT ON THIS STEEP CLIFF WHERE IT RISES FROM THE KINNERET, WHAT YOU CALL THE SEA OF GALILEE.

BY THESE LAST TWO DAYS IN 1967, THE SYRIANS HAD HEARD THAT THE JORDANIAN AND EGYPTIAN ARMIES HAD BEEN DEFEATED.

THEY KNEW THEY COULD NOT HOLD BACK THE ISRAELI ARMY FOR LONG, SO THEY DECIDED TO PLAY A GAME WITH INTERNATIONAL POLITICS.

DAMASCUS

THE SYRIAN GOVERNMENT ANNOUNCED THAT THE ISRAELIS HAD ALREADY ADVANCED PAST THE CLIFFS AND WERE MARCHING TOWARDS DAMASCUS.

THEY HOPED THAT ONCE THE INTERNATIONAL COMMUNITY HEARD THIS FALSE REPORT THEY WOULD PRESSURE ISRAEL INTO A CEASE-FIRE.

UNITED NATIONS

AND IT WORKED. WITHIN 24 HOURS ISRAEL WAS COMPELLED TO STOP FIGHTING.

BUT WHAT HAPPENED *DURING* THAT 24 HOURS WAS VERY INTERESTING.

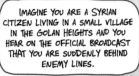

IMAGINE YOU ARE A SYRIAN CITIZEN LIVING IN A SMALL VILLAGE IN THE GOLAN HEIGHTS AND YOU HEAR ON THE OFFICIAL BROADCAST THAT YOU ARE SUDDENLY BEHIND ENEMY LINES.

WHAT WOULD YOU DO? YOU WOULD TAKE WHAT YOU CAN CARRY ON YOUR BACK AND EVACUATE!

AND BY THE WAY, ISRAELIS DID THE SAME THING LAST SUMMER WHEN HEZBOLLAH WAS FIRING ROCKETS OVER THE LEBANESE BORDER.

200,000 ISRAELIS MOVED TO CENTRAL ISRAEL UNTIL THE FIGHTING STOPPED AND THEN RETURNED TO THEIR HOMES.

THE SYRIAN PEOPLE DID THE SAME, AND WE'RE TALKING HALF A MILLION PEOPLE, ONLY THEY COULD NOT RETURN TO THEIR HOMES BECAUSE WE CAPTURED THE TERRITORY.

THIS JUNE IT WILL HAVE BEEN FORTY YEARS SINCE THEY HAVE NOT BEEN ABLE TO RETURN.

NOW THE SYRIAN *ARMY*, THAT WAS A DIFFERENT STORY.

WHEN THE OFFICERS HEARD THE TROUBLING NEWS THAT THEY WERE FIGHTING ON THE RIDGE BUT WERE NOW BEHIND ISRAELI UNITS, THEY PANICKED.

Analyze

(1) This graphic essay focuses on the Golan Heights, which is a disputed area arranged between and within the borders of Israel and Syria—land that has been the center of a longstanding heated political struggle between Arab and Israeli forces. Use the Internet to familiarize yourself with the recent history of the Golan Heights, from the Six-Day War in 1967 to the present. Based on your research, do you believe Glidden's graphic travelogue fairly depicts recent events in the Golan Heights?

(2) "How to Understand Israel" is arranged, in part, as an argument. Glidden attempts to explore political issues evenhandedly. Is she successful? What is her position on proper ownership of Golan Heights? What attitudes or opinions is she trying to pass on to the reader?

(3) Glidden explores the aims of propaganda—specifically a heavily biased use of media to shape public opinion. She believes that the film at the Golan Magic tourist center is propaganda because it consciously presents a political argument as unbiased history. In this context, explore the problems with propaganda and how they contribute to longstanding conflicts. In your opinion, what is the difference between a proper argument—which seeks to influence public opinion—and propaganda?

(4) Propaganda is used to manage the political views of an audience by coloring historic or newsworthy events without acknowledging a bias. By this definition, most countries use some form of propaganda. Identify three forms of propaganda—film, magazine articles, TV shows, websites, newspaper articles, and so on—that are used in your country.

Explore

(1) The main figure in this comic, "Sarah," is intentionally presented with minimal facial detail and slightly androgynous features, with the hope that readers will more easily imagine themselves in Sarah's situation. Do you find that you can project your experience more easily on to figures with minimal detail (such as in "How to Understand Israel") as compared to figures that have greater specificity of detail (such as in "Love Me Forever!")?

(2) How does the artwork (the soft colors, the empty environments, the facial expressions and bodily gestures of the participants) help readers to put aside pre-existing beliefs about the Golan Heights and explore the comic with a relatively open mind? Do Glidden's illustrations of the Golan Heights suggest attitudes of conflict, peace, leisure, boredom, or turmoil?

(3) The color palette of the Golan Heights, with its soft browns and yellows, appears in sharp contrast to the deep reds and blues of the presentation theater and its film. How does Glidden establish two different moods with the use of these color sets?

(4)   Though Glidden was not born in Israel, as a young adult she took a "Birthright Israel" trip to Tel Aviv, Jerusalem, and the Golan Heights to better understand the land of her ancestors. In your own life, how do the traditions, beliefs, and history of your ancestors shape your own present identity?

LEELA CORMAN

Unterzakhn

Leela Corman is a self-described "illustrator, cartoonist, and Middle Eastern dancer" who studied illustration, painting, and printmaking at Massachusetts College of Art. As an undergraduate student, she self-published numerous issues of *Flimflam*, a mini-comic. Corman followed that up with *Subway Series*, by Alternative Books, and had work published in anthologies in the United States, France, Spain, and Portugal, as well as provided illustrations for the *New York Times* and *Family Circle*. Her book *Unterzakhn*, which examines the lives of twin Jewish girls growing up in New York's Lower East Side in the early 1900s, is her most famous work.

Identity

Identity

Leela Corman: *Unterzakhn*   61

Identity

Analyze

(1) *Unterzakhn* is far less dependent on dialogue than many of the other selections in this book. Corman admits that having a lot of dialogue will "push the pictures out of the way." What other effects does such limited dialogue have on a reader? Does it have any effect on the pacing of the story? The meaning?

(2) The word "unterzakhn" is Yiddish for "underthings." Certainly this refers to underwear (in fact, at the book launch, the publisher gave away *Unterzakhn* underwear!), but what else might this term refer to? And why is it important that it is a Yiddish word? Why do you think she uses Yiddish terms, such as "pritze," meaning both "whore" and "spoiled brat," throughout the text? What does it mean that both girls learn a word like "pritze" but neither is quite sure what it means?

(3) Fanya is told by the female obstetrician, "It's men's drives, you see, that keep Woman reproducing constantly, like a breed cow. Sexual slavery awaits the woman who allows a man to entrap her, either in marriage or in a quick and ugly gutter union." How do you react to such a statement? Is this being said as an act of surrender or as a way to fortify the young girl and prepare her for the world of contradictory systems of sex and money?

(4) Why do you think this story was included in the Identity section of this textbook? Consider issues of family, religion, and community. What other sections could it easily fit into? In your opinion, is a work of literature stronger when it focuses primarily on one theme or on multiple themes?

Explore

(1) In an interview with Forward.com, Corman says, "Pictures are central. I'm a visual artist, not a novelist." What do you see as important differences between a visual artist and a novelist or short story writer? What are the important similarities? To what degree should a graphic novelist be either, neither, or both?

(2) Sex depicted on the page can entice the reader with images of pleasure, or it can alienate the reader with images of discomfort. What reaction do you have to the sexual situations in this story? What cues in the story help create that reaction?

(3) *Unterzakhn* has been called a fable. Look up the definition of this word, and perhaps find some examples of it. Why is this story called a fable? Of what use are fables today?

(4) Largeheartedboy.com has a Book Notes series where authors create and then discuss a music playlist that relates to one of their recently published books. Visit the April 4, 2012, entry by Leela Corman, and listen to music selections she makes (at least those you can find). Read her rationale for the choices. How do these experiences shed light back on the story? What new understandings or insights emerge? What new questions do you have?

Leela Corman: *Unterzakhn*

Men and Women

In a series of bestselling books on relationships and personal growth, Dr. John Gray suggested that men and women were so different they might have originated on their own planets: men from Mars, and women from Venus. Through detailed examples, he put forth an argument that many factors contributed to our cultural sense of identity being highly rooted in gender: differences in concepts of masculinity and femininity, biological differences, cultural expectations, and so forth. Through these books Dr. Gray contributed to a longstanding discussion on the meaning of gender, the role it plays in identity, and the pressures it often places on relationships. But Dr. Gray was by no means the first—or most rigorous—popular writer to explore the connection between gender and identity. In 1963, Betty Friedan initiated the second wave of feminism in America with her book *The Feminine Mystique*, which explored social limitations of roles available to women. In 1855, Robert Browning's poetry book *Men and Women* delved into the complex relationship between men and women during the time of industrialization, when some liberals were starting to murmur about women's rights. Two hundred years before Browning, Anne Bradstreet explored the meaning and limitations of women's roles through her poetry. Before this, there was Shakespeare, Chaucer, Plato, and dozens of others dating likely back to the early ages of recorded history.

For good reason, then, we've included a section on gender in this textbook, as contemporary visual authors are drawn to the subject as well. But gender is an umbrella term encompassing many areas of exploration, such as the idea of power as it applies to men and women, the concept of gender as it applies to roles within the workplace and the family, the legal limitations as they apply to gender, social concepts of masculinity and femininity, and the ways in which emerging roles for men and women sustain, advance, change, or subvert longstanding ideas about gender.

The texts in this selection add to this ongoing conversation. "La Brea Woman" by Martin Cendreda concerns modes of masculinity as they are passed from father to son. Kevin Huizenga's "Pulverize," too, focuses on young men as they connect through their experiences in violent, digital environments. In contrast, Vanessa Davis's "In the Rough" explores ways that the institution of marriage can intrude on a woman's independence. Brent Eric Anderson's "The Hero" explores situations in which young boys are forced to act the part of adults, playing both father and mother, in how they care for others.

The narratives in this section continue the discussion of one of literature's enduring themes. At their best, such as in "Cecil and Jordan in New York" by Gabrielle Bell, the authors lower us with ropes down into the midst of identity so we can better see how concepts of gender help form the essence of personality and partially define the roles we inhabit through life.

VANESSA DAVIS

"In The Rough"

Vanessa Davis is a confessional artist, with most of the ideas for her comics coming directly from her diary. Her work has appeared in the *New York Times*, *Dissent*, *Vice*, and *Best American Comics*. In 2010, Davis published *Make Me a Woman*, an auto-biographical collection of visual essays, sketches, and journal excerpts, to critical praise.

Men and Women

Men and Women

Analyze

(1) Traditionally only women wear engagement rings to show their commitment to the relationship. Before the wedding, men do not wear a ring. In your opinion, is this tradition—in which only one gender wears a ring before marriage—a custom that no longer matches your understanding of men and women's roles? Or does it still hold value?

(2) Another observation raised by the comic is the connection between an engagement ring and its cost. The traditional stone for an engagement ring is the diamond, a jewel that can cost upward of a few thousand dollars. In your opinion, does the tradition of the ring too strongly commercialize engagement, focusing attention on the cost of the ring rather than on the depth of a couple's love and commitment?

(3) The comic suggests that "dating is private" whereas marriage is a public commitment. Based on your own experience, is this observation still true: is dating primarily a private endeavor? Or has culture changed—with Facebook, Instagram, and so on—so that dating is not primarily a private endeavor anymore?

(4) Lastly, the wedding ring for both men and women, as explained in the comic, can be a symbol of ownership, indicating that this man or woman is "owned" by another. How do you feel about this tradition?

Explore

(1) If you were to replace the tradition of the engagement/wedding ring with a new custom to show commitment between two people, what elements would this new custom have?

(2) From a legal standpoint, marriage is a contract between two people for mutual support. This contract could easily be accomplished by two people visiting a website and filling out and signing a form to legally solidify their intentions. In your opinion, would anything be lost if a wedding service were performed via a webpage and not in a church, temple, park, or home?

(3) "In The Rough" is a visual argument in which illustrations contribute to the author's message. What would be lost if this argument were arranged as a traditional, verbal argument (with paragraphs and no pictures)? What would be gained?

(4) Write an essay in which you explore or challenge the social value of one long-standing custom in contemporary society. You may choose to explore or challenge the custom of giving a wedding ring only to women, burying people in a cemetery, receiving a diploma to show mastery of a subject, throwing a wild twenty-first birthday party, giving a child the father's surname (last name), hosting a birthday party each year, or any other longstanding custom that interests you.

DEBBIE DRESCHSLER

"The Dead of Winter"

At an early age, Debbie Dreschsler was drawn to drawing. As a teenager, she drew horses and celebrities and created psychedelic posters using Day-Glo paints. As an adult, she developed a career as an illustrator, both for children's books and for popular periodicals such as the *Los Angeles Times* and *Conde Nast Traveler*. Presently she lives in Santa Rosa, just north of San Francisco.

THE DEAD OF WINTER

ME AND MY BOYFRIEND DROPPED OUT OF COLLEGE BECAUSE OF WHAT A WASTE IT WAS. I THOUGHT WE WERE GOING TO LIVE TOGETHER BUT HE MOVED BACK TO HIS PARENTS' IN WHITE PLAINS SO HE COULD SELL VACUUM CLEANERS DOOR-TO-DOOR AND EARN ENOUGH TO BUY A NEW CAR. I WAS LIVING AT MY PARENTS' AND SELLING ART SUPPLIES WHEN I FOUND OUT I WAS PREGNANT. ONE NIGHT, WHEN THE REST OF MY FAMILY WAS OUT, I CALLED TO TELL HIM THE NEWS.

SO, ALSO, I'M PREGNANT.

YEAH. WELL. ALSO. SOMEONE HAS TO GO WITH ME. TO THE CLINIC. FOR THE ABORTION. YOU KNOW. JUST IN CASE.

YEAH. SURE. LISTEN, I GOTTA GO.

OH GREAT! I KNEW THIS WOULD HAPPEN!

SEE, LIL, THE THING IS, I CAN'T OR I WON'T MAKE MY QUOTA THIS MONTH. YOU UNDERSTAND, RIGHT? ANYWAY, YOU'LL BE FINE.

ME, TOO. BYE.

© 1996 Debbie Drechsler

I KEPT HOPING HE'D CHANGE HIS MIND BUT I GUESS HE NEVER DID. SO I FINALLY HAD TO ASK MY SISTER PEARL. RIGHT AWAY I KNEW IT WAS A BIG MISTAKE.

SO, WHERE IS HE IF HE'S SO IN LOVE WITH YOU, HUH?

SHUT UP, PEARL! HE'S GOT IMPORTANT STUFF TO DO!

YEAH! LIKE BUY A NEW CAR! BIG DEAL!

JUST SHUT UP, OK?

ANYWAY, WE FINALLY MADE IT TO BUFFALO, WHICH IS WHERE THE CLINIC WAS.

THERE IT IS.

IT DOESN'T LOOK SO BAD.

C'MON. LET'S GET IT OVER WITH.

YEAH. I GUESS. OKAY.

THE LAST THING I SAW BEFORE MY ABORTION WAS PEARL IN THE WAITING ROOM, SURROUNDED BY THE BOYFRIENDS OF THE OTHER GIRLS WHO WERE HAVING IT DONE. MY BOYFRIEND NEVER EVEN CALLED TO WISH ME GOOD LUCK OR ANYTHING.

THE WHOLE TIME OF THE PROCEDURE I HAD THE STRANGE FEELING OF IT HAPPENING TO SOMEONE ELSE, AND I WAS JUST THERE TO OBSERVE.

WHEN IT WAS OVER THEY TOOK ME TO THIS OTHER ROOM WHERE I WAS SUPPOSED TO REST. ALL I WANTED WAS TO GET OUT OF THAT PLACE AND PUT IT ALL BEHIND ME.

OH! I DON'T NEED TO REST! I'M FINE! SO I'LL JUST GO HOME, OK?

WE'D LIKE YOU TO REST, JUST FOR AWHILE.

DO I HAVE TO?

HERE'S YOUR BLANKET.

WOO HOO HOO

WOO HOO HOO OOOOO WOO HOO

YEAH, RIGHT. THIS IS REAL RESTFUL. UH HUH.

YOUR SISTER'S BEEN VERY WORRIED ABOUT YOU SO HERE SHE IS TO KEEP YOU COMPANY, OK?

HOW SOON CAN I GO?

HI PEARL.

I DIDN'T REALLY BELIEVE PEARL WAS ACTUALLY WORRIED ABOUT ME, BUT YOU KNOW? IT WASN'T SO BAD TO SEE HER JUST THEN.

YOU OK?

YEAH.

WHAT'S WRONG WITH HER?

ALL I KNOW IS SHE'S DRIVING ME CRAZY!

I BELIEVE IT!

HOO WOO WOO HOO OOOO

LATER

HOO HOO HOOOOO

LILY, YOU CAN GO NOW. DON'T FORGET TO MAKE A FOLLOW-UP APPOINTMENT WITH YOUR GYNECOLOGIST.

I WON'T.

WELL, THEN, GOOD LUCK.

THANKS

PEARL AND I DIDN'T TALK MUCH ON THE WAY HOME.

BOY, I LOVE THIS SONG!

WELL, I HATE IT.

FIGURES!

2

PEARL HAD HER OWN APARTMENT SO SHE TOOK ME TO OUR PARENTS' HOUSE FIRST.

BETTER DROP ME OFF HERE. THEY THINK I WORKED TODAY.

OH, OK.

REMEMBER! DON'T TELL ANYONE, OK?

I WON'T.

PROMISE?

PROMISE. CROSS MY HEART.

THANKS PEARL. FOR EVERYTHING.

NO SWEAT.

THAT NIGHT I HAD A DREAM...

...WHERE I WAS ALL ALONE IN AN UNFAMILIAR PLACE.

I WAS DESPERATELY LOOKING FOR SOMETHING.

MY LIFE DEPENDED ON FINDING IT...

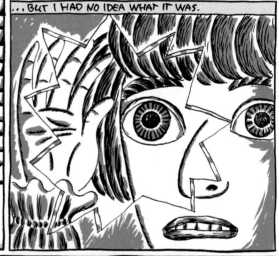

...BUT I HAD NO IDEA WHAT IT WAS.

WHEN I'D FINALLY GIVEN UP ON EVER FINDING IT...

...I SAW THE STRANGEST THING. SOMEHOW I KNEW THAT IT WAS WHAT I'D BEEN LOOKING FOR.

I WAS REALLY HAPPY AND HORRIBLY SAD ALL AT ONCE. I WANTED SO BADLY TO TOUCH IT OR HOLD IT. OR SOMETHING.

BUT I GUESS I SCARED IT...

...AND THEN I COULDN'T FIND IT AT ALL, BECAUSE THERE WERE A MILLION STARS AND IT COULD'VE BEEN ANY ONE OF THEM.

WHEN I WOKE UP I WAS CRYING HARDER THAN I EVER HAD SINCE I WAS A LITTLE KID. I CRIED AND CRIED AND CRIED...

...AND THEN IT STOPPED, JUST LIKE THAT. BUT NO WAY COULD I GET BACK TO SLEEP.

I GOT THIS CRAZY URGE TO GO OUTSIDE.

5

IT HAD STOPPED SNOWING AND THE WORLD LOOKED SO BEAUTIFUL THAT IT SEEMED UNREAL TO ME, LIKE A DREAM OR SOME FAIRY TALE.

WOW!

I LOOKED UP, HALF HOPING TO SEE THE THING FROM MY DREAM BUT ALL I SAW WAS A SKY FULL OF STARS.

THEN, JUST IN CASE IT WAS REALLY UP THERE, I BLEW IT A KISS, THE WAY MY MOM USED TO, WHEN WE WERE BABIES, AND SHE HAD TO GO AWAY.

SMACK!

I WAITED A LONG TIME FOR A SIGN OR SOMETHING BUT THERE WASN'T ONE. I KNEW IT PROBABLY HATED ME. ANYWAY, WHO COULD BLAME IT?

I WISHED I COULD EXPLAIN WHY I DID IT, BUT EVERYTHING WAS SO COMPLICATED. THERE WAS NO WAY.

I'M SORRY.

BY THEN I WAS FREEZING, SO I TURNED AROUND AND WENT BACK INTO THE HOUSE.

END

Analyze

(1) From a visual standpoint, the individuals in this comic share many presentation values with cartoon characters. Lily, for example, has enlarged eyes and very little facial definition, and her limbs bend as though they were made of rubber, without anatomically precise knees or elbows. In your opinion, do you see the individuals in this comic more as fully developed, realistic characters or as the type of caricatures that often inhabit cartoons or the funny pages of a newspaper? Why?

(2) The visual style of "The Dead of Winter" appears to be influenced by German Expressionism. Expressionist painters often presented the world from a highly personal perspective, distorting the landscape to emphasize the emotional experience of the artist. The dream sequence in "The Dead of Winter" absorbs many aspects of Expressionism—the curved buildings and doorways, the distorted perspective of sidewalks and streets, and Lily's sensation of floating. How does the Expressionist presentation of this sequence change the emotional textures of the story?

(3) In your opinion, why does Lily so vigorously defend her boyfriend to her sister Pearl—especially when her boyfriend appears unconcerned with Lily's struggles? Is Lily concerned with how her sister will treat her boyfriend the next time she sees him? Is she concerned with how Pearl views her? Is she trying to justify various decisions (quitting college, working a low-paying job, etc.) simply so she feels better about herself?

(4) In the comic's final panels, how is Lily changed by her dream and her experience outside at night? In your opinion, will these experiences have a lasting impact on her? If so, how will the experience of the dream and the walk afterward stay with her?

Explore

(1) In this comic, Lily is surrounded by people who don't understand her needs and struggles. Where does Lily feel most understood? How does Lily contribute to her problem of feeling distant from and her sense of not being understood by those around her?

(2) "The Dead of Winter" uses a single accent color of cerulean blue to texture its images. In your opinion, why did the artist use this color? What emotional or atmospheric values does this color bring to the "feel" of the comic?

(3) This story suggests that meaningful emotional experiences can be explored and digested through dream images while a person sleeps. For two weeks, keep a dream diary. As soon as you awaken each morning, write down each of your dreams, using vivid descriptions and concrete language. At the end of the second week, review your diary entries to see whether you can make meaningful connections between your waking life and your dream life.

(4) This story presents a difficult experience in Lily's adult life, one in which she "cried and cried and cried." Write an essay that tells the story of a low point in your life as a young adult—after age fifteen. How did the experience change you? How do aspects of the experience stay with you today?

GABRIELLE BELL

"Cecil and Jordan in New York"

Gabrielle Bell was born in England, but at the age of two, she moved to Northern California with her mother. She attended Humboldt State University and City College of San Francisco, where she studied art. In 1998 she began to self-publish her comics in yearly collections. Her art fluctuates between surrealism and realist line drawings. More so than most contemporary comic artists, her understanding of narrative is strongly related to the traditions of the American short story. As such, our textbook includes more than one entry by Gabrielle Bell. Presently she lives in Brooklyn, New York.

We arrived in Brooklyn on a snowy December night.

MAKE A RIGHT! I MEAN A LEFT! MAYBE WE SHOULD JUST STOP.

WE'RE NOT MOVING!

We stayed with our old high school friend Gladys, in her tiny, one-room studio. It was cluttered with furniture that all seemed to have been found on the street.

MY BOYFRIEND IS GOING TO BE STAYING HERE ON SATURDAY.

Jordan was able to get a couple of screenings for his film, but they didn't look promising.

WHERE IS 'SHEEPSHEAD BAY'?

IT'S AT A PORNO THEATRE BUT I GUESS THEY SHOW REGULAR FILMS TOO.

we've been at this for so long that all his shows mean to me anymore is that we'll be moving equipment at three in the morning.

DON'T YOU HAVE THE KEYS?

Our savings were drying up, so Jordan found seasonal work at a toy store, and I set about getting some temporary housing.

THERE'S A THOUSAND DOLLAR DEPOSIT, AND I TAKE OUT A HUNDRED FOR EACH THING YOU BREAK.

Until I could find an affordable place, I did my best to keep out of Gladys' way.

On the third day of the blizzard, the alternate side parking suspension was lifted, and all of the money we made on our tour went towards a parking ticket.

Jordan worked thirteen hour shifts every day, and was always in a bad mood.

...AND WHEN THERE AREN'T ANY TOYS TO BE WRAPPED I HAVE TO WRAP EMPTY BOXES FOR DISPLAY.

DO YOU THINK IT'S LATE ENOUGH TO GO BACK TO GLADYS' HOUSE?

He did get us invited to some work parties.

SO ARE YOU IN IT?

NO, BUT I HELPED A LITTLE WITH THE EDITING.

ARE YOU A FILMMAKER TOO?

NO, I'M JUST HIS GIRLFRIEND.

MERRY CHR

I didn't have proper footwear for the snow, so I bought some new boots, which gave me such bad blisters that it hurt to walk.

But it wasn't like I had anywhere to go.

84

And that is why I transformed myself into a chair.

I stood on the sidewalk and waited.

Soon a man came and took me home.

He showed me off to his friends.

IT'S A BIT RICKETY, BUT IT'S A GOOD CHAIR.

GOOD SCORE!

When he was away, I'd turn myself back into a girl, and lounge around his house.

When he came home I became a chair again.

I wondered how Jordan was doing.

I wondered how the car was.

I decided I wouldn't be missed much.

But the days slip by so pleasantly that such thoughts don't linger long in my mind.

Sometimes, there are close calls.

But then, I've never felt so useful.

Men and Women

Analyze

(1) A color palette is a selection of colors—or "color swatches"—that an artist uses to define the physical and emotional space of a comic. In "Cecil and Jordan in New York," Bell uses a palette of darker tones—dark reds, blues slanting toward gray, twilight greens, skin tones illuminated by low light, and so on—to define and harmonize the world. What emotions are suggested by this particular combination of colors?

(2) This comic is mostly comprised of "long shots"—that is, panels featuring the full figure of each character—that create visual distance between the characters and the reader, much like video images from a security camera or footage used in a newscast. There are no close-up panels focused on a character's expression or facial composition. In your opinion, why did the author choose to present the story this way? How do these long shots add to the meaning or emotional space of the comic?

(3) The woman in this comic is never formally given a name, though based on the title one can assume it is Cecil. After Cecil turns into a chair, she assumes human form only when she is alone. In your opinion, why can she be her authentic self only when no one else is around?

(4) As the chair, Cecil's job is to literally support the man who found her. The caption in the last panel pairs the line "I've never felt so useful" with the image of Cecil as the chair. How are we to read this line: as the literal truth, with dry humor, with biting irony, or as a tragic-yet-straightforward statement about gender roles in America? With this in mind, what is the social statement Bell is trying to make through her story?

Explore

(1) Cecil has two significant relationships with men. In the first, she follows her boyfriend to New York. In the second, she lives partly as a chair with the man in his apartment. In what ways are these two relationships similar? In what ways are they different?

(2) Jordan is a young artist on the verge of failure: he is a filmmaker who can't support himself by making films. In your opinion, how much support should society offer young artists during their early career years? And what obligation do artists have to a society that has supported them?

(3) This is the first comic for which Bell used color. In this textbook, locate a comic of black-and-white line art (such as "The Hero" by Brent Eric Anderson) for which you will develop your own color palette. A color palette is a set of color swatches that defines emotional space and harmonizes the visual presentation. Select up to eight color swatches that will establish a palette. In a one-page paper, present your color swatches and explain your rationale for selecting them.

(4) Cecil sees herself primarily in a role of support for men and therefore becomes a chair, which is an object that provides support. This image demeans Cecil's personhood and creates a situation in which she is *literally* less than human. With this in mind, write a short personal essay that explores a moment in which you *felt* less than human, and include an examination of the underlying causes and your reaction to the situation. What would you say you learned from this experience?

AVRIL AND PETIT-ROULET

"63 Rue de la Grange aux Belles"

François Avril was born in France. He attended one of the four major art schools in Paris: Ècole Nationale Supérieure des Arts Appliqués et des Métiers d'Art. In addition to comics, Avril creates illustrations for magazines, advertisements, and children's books. His work has been exhibited in galleries in Paris, Amsterdam, Strasbourg, and Tokyo.

Also born in Paris, Philippe Petit-Roulet published his first comics in the early 1970s. Since then, his work has appeared in TV commercials, short films, newspapers, magazine advertisements, and children's books. His comic illustrations are regularly featured in *The New Yorker*.

PETIT-ROULET

63 Rue de la Grange aux Belles_

Men and Women

Men and Women

Men and Women

Men and Women

Analyze

(1) This comic is purely visual, conveying a story without verbal dialogue or narration. Dialogue is communicated through pictograms and icons. How is the experience of reading this comic different from that of reading a comic that includes traditional dialogue and narration? How does the silence of this narrative change the way you understand and relate to these characters?

(2) The two central figures—the man with yellow hair and the man with brown hair—are outcasts at the cocktail party. This is particularly true for the man with yellow hair. He approaches attractive women, only to be turned down by each one. He also attempts to discuss art with intellectuals—they appear to be discussing Paul Gauguin and Henri Matisse—only to be rejected by them as well. In your opinion, why is the man with yellow hair so unpopular at the party? How do you understand his personality based on his gestures and his dialogue of pictograms?

(3) The brown-haired man is continually surprised and embarrassed to find couples engaged in sexual activity. What does this experience mean for him?

(4) As the comic ends, the yellow-haired man is speaking freely about cars and the brown-haired man is sitting happily (not dancing) beside a quiet woman he met earlier in the night. What do the final panels mean for both of these men?

Explore

(1) On the second page of the comic—as the man with yellow hair explains his intentions to approach the lady in green—write out verbal dialogue for each panel. Does the man speak formally, casually, with slang expressions, with a halting insecurity, with artificial confidence? How does language change the "feel" of the comic? Does language make the yellow-haired man easier to know? Or are you able to imagine a richer inner life for him without the intrusion of language?

(2) The characters in this comic are rendered as flat caricatures (with little facial detail), the type of drawings one might find in funny pages of a newspaper, yet these characters are presented with darkly real, adult situations: casual sexual encounters, romantic isolation, and group exclusion. Do you have feelings of empathy or sympathy for these cartoon caricatures? If so, why?

(3) Using only a visual medium (such as illustration, photography, video) create an essay without words that narrates a recent experience that was important to you. Make sure your visual essay in some way communicates the meaning of this experience as you understand it.

(4) In an essay, narrate an event in which you were excluded. How did the event change you? What did you learn from it?

BRENT ERIC ANDERSON

"The Hero"

Brent Eric Anderson grew up in a house where his mother disapproved of comics, asking her son instead to read classic children's literature like *Treasure Island*. Despite her concerns, by the time he was in junior high, he'd found comics at the local drugstore, his favorite of which was *Fantastic Four*. As an adult, Anderson found a career in illustration and comics. His credits include work on *X-Men*, *Green Lantern*, and *Astro City*.

ANDERSON

In the summer of 1964 i was nine. My mom and dad had divorced the year before. My dad wanted to take me on a fishing trip with him—to do the things fathers and sons were supposed to do, i guess.

It was three o'clock in the morning when he picked me up. i don't know how far away the lake was 'cuz i slept the whole way. The sun was just rising when we got there.

I hadn't yet learned to swim, so riding in an overloaded fishing boat over a lake had me wide awake.

The Hero

Men and Women

BY NOON WE ALL NEEDED A BREAK.

OUR DADS WANTED TO FISH THAT AFTER-NOON, SO THEY TOOK US WITH THEM.

I WASN'T VERY GOOD AT LEARNING TO FISH, BUT DANNY HAD A GOOD TIME.

I SAID THE RIVER IS A NO-NO!

THIS WAS WHAT FATHERS AND SONS WERE SUP-POSED TO DO TOGETHER.

That evening while supper was cooking, i went to explore the sandbar in the mouth of the shallow river.

I found some baby birds in a hollow tree stump.

But i couldn't see them very well.

It would be another month before i got my first pair of glasses.

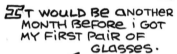

awk?

awwk awwwk

RAHK RAHK

RAHK

Men and Women

Men and Women

· THIS STORY IS DEDICATED TO MY FATHER WHEREVER HE MAY BE·

Analyze

(1) "The Hero"—a story of divorce, danger, and death—explores the themes of survival and loss. Discuss loss as it pertains to both the narrator and his father in this story, and explore how these events perhaps frame a type of family survival.

(2) Late in the story, the narrator discovers what the bird really wanted: "It wanted food. Not a stick." In what ways are other characters lacking what they need?

(3) At the end of the final panel, Anderson notes, "This story is dedicated to my father wherever he may be." Because this story is mostly focused on loss, why do you think he dedicates it to his father?

(4) The story is called "The Hero," but at the end the narrator decides that he wasn't one because "no one ever called me one." In what sense are the narrator's action's heroic? What has he learned about himself—or his family—by the time his father returns him to his mother's care at the end?

Explore

(1) A social ritual—like a Friday night bowling date or a Sunday walk along the beach—is an activity that a family does repeatedly, with the events in it arranged in the same general order. In this story, fishing is a social ritual that the fathers enact to engender closeness with their sons. On a blank sheet of paper, make a list of rituals that your parents enact to create a feeling of closeness in your family.

(2) Some of the most emotional drawings in the story occur when the narrator loses the baby bird to the river. In one panel, the narrator, as the bird sinks, stares directly at the reader. Examine the composition of this drawing. How is emotion conveyed? Which aspects of the narrator's face best convey feeling?

(3) This story, set in 1964, presents traditional roles of masculinity: fathers and sons attempt to find closeness by camping and fishing in the wilderness. In terms of gender roles, many things have changed since 1964. In a short essay of personal exploration, examine how gender roles were defined in your family. Did your parents have different expectations for boys and girls: their interests, their clothes, their hobbies, their toys, their abilities in school or in sports? Or did your parents have a single set of gender-neutral expectations? How did ideas of gender in your family help form your present personality and compose an image of the person you aspire to be after college?

(4) In some ways, this is a story about failed care: the father fails by leaving his nine-year-old son to watch over Danny; the narrator fails by letting the baby bird drown; the narrator also fails by allowing Danny to wade in the shallows. In a short personal essay, narrate an experience in which you failed at some important task. What did you learn from this experience? How did it change you?

MARTIN CENDREDA

"La Brea Woman"

Born in Los Angeles, Martin Cendreda makes his living in the world of animation. Since 2000, he has worked on roughly one dozen TV shows, including *South Park*, *Fairly Odd Parents*, and *Adventure Time*, as an animator, character designer, colorist, or director. He holds a BA in landscape architecture from UC Berkeley and a BFA in animation from UCLA School of Film. His comics appear in various journals and magazines, including *Mome*, and have been anthologized in *The Best American Comics*.

Men and Women

9 YEARS AGO, CHARLES ("CHAS" SINCE CHILDHOOD) GAS MARRIED HIS FIRST AND ONLY GIRLFRIEND, MARLENE. THEY HAD A CIVIL CEREMONY FOLLOWED BY A BACK-YARD BARBECUE ATTENDED BY A FEW CLOSE FRIENDS, BUT NO RELATIVES.

OUR WEEKEND'S ALMOST UP, TOMMY BOY. I GOT TO TAKE YOU BACK TO YOUR MOM'S TONITE. YOU WANNA GO TO THE TAR PITS TODAY, SEE US SOME WOOLY MAMMOTHS?

OKAY.

42 YEARS FROM NOW, THOMAS WILL BE SIGNING HIS OWN DIVORCE PAPERS ON THIS VERY TABLE, WHICH HE INHERITS A YEAR BEFORE HIS FATHER DIES OF CANCER. THE CLAW FEET UNNERVED HIM HIS ENTIRE LIFE.

YOUR MOTHER HAS YOU NEXT WEEKEND, BUT I'VE GOT YOU FOR SPRING BREAK.

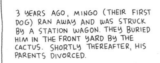

3 YEARS AGO, MINGO (THEIR FIRST DOG) RAN AWAY AND WAS STRUCK BY A STATION WAGON. THEY BURIED HIM IN THE FRONT YARD BY THE CACTUS. SHORTLY THEREAFTER, HIS PARENTS DIVORCED.

I GOTTA PEE FIRST.

SEEMS LIKE YESTERDAY... SEEMS LIKE FOREVER...

WANNA STOP FOR A CHOCOLATE MILKSHAKE?

YUP.

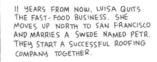

11 YEARS FROM NOW, LUISA QUITS THE FAST-FOOD BUSINESS. SHE MOVES UP NORTH TO SAN FRANCISCO AND MARRIES A SWEDE NAMED PETR. THEY START A SUCCESSFUL ROOFING COMPANY TOGETHER.

WELL, LOOKIT THAT. GUESS I NEED AN OIL CHANGE SOON.

Martin Cendreda: "La Brea Woman"

Men and Women

About 50,000 years ago, in this very spot, crude oil began to seep out of the ground, forming huge pools of tar. A variety of pre-historic animals (from saber-toothed cats to American mastodons) became trapped and eventually died in these "tar pits". Their bones were discovered here in the early 1900's.

Y'know they found a lady in there once. Not like you and me. 8,000 years ago she fell in. Got some of her bones inside the museum. I wonder what her story was? Heh heh!

20 years from now, on the night before he died, Robert would have a dream about wandering around a used bookstore where the smell of tar was both vivid and unmistakable. The mortician thought the smile a bit disconcerting.

How about we eat our sandwiches at the top of the hill?

Okie doke.

Also, 20 years from now, Thomas would return here with his own 8-year-old son, Artie, who would roll down this hill 6 times before vomiting in his father's lap.

I adult, 1 child please.

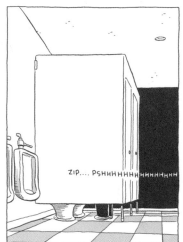

Men and Women

I BETTER GET YOU FED. YOUR MOTHER WILL KILL ME IF I BRING YOU BACK TO HER PLACE WITHOUT ANY DINNER.

AFTER THAT, YOU CAN HAVE A PIECE OF THAT DINOSAUR CANDY.

AMBER·KANDY
IT'S A PRE·HISTORIC TREAT!!!

REAL EDIBLE CANDY THAT LOOKS JUST LIKE FOSSILIZED AMBER. WITH INSECTS YOU CAN REALLY EAT!!

IT'S LIKE THEY'RE FROZEN, EH? ... FROZEN IN TIME.

1 YEAR FROM NOW, TO THE DAY, AT THIS VERY STATION, "RED" (AS HE WAS KNOWN ON THE STREET) WOULD DIE FROM A METH-AMPHETAMINE OVERDOSE. HIS BODY LAY HIDDEN IN THE BACK BUSHES FOR THREE AND A HALF DAYS.

NOPE, SORRY. I DON'T HAVE ANY CHANGE.

4 YEARS AGO, ANOUSH'S DOG (SNOOPY II) RAN OFF IN THE MIDDLE OF THE NIGHT AND NEVER RETURNED. HE HAS WORKED EVERY NIGHT SHIFT SINCE THEN, HOPING SHE'LL COME BACK.

FILL UP ON 3. AND A PACK OF CAMELS TOO, PLEASE.

CAMELS

SHIT, IT'S NOT MY FAULT! HE FELL ASLEEP BEFORE WE HAD A CHANCE TO EAT, **OKAY**? LOOK, I DON'T WANT TO FIGHT AGAIN. I'LL PICK HIM UP AGAIN IN TWO WEEKS. G'NIGHT.

mart

Analyze

(1) The "gutter," the thin white space between two panels is particularly relevant in this comic as it, too, suggests a passing of time. In some comics, particularly in action sequences, the gutter separates drawn images by a second or two. In "La Brea Woman" many minutes pass between most of the drawings. The gutters here, then, represent the passage of a significant period of time. Many important moments are left out of the comic and left to readers to imagine, such as the conversation Charles and his son have after visiting La Brea Tar Pits and the moment Charles says goodnight to his son. Reread "La Brea Woman" with an eye toward exploring those moments not depicted in the comic. In your opinion, which is the most interesting moment left out of the text?

(2) Both Charles and his son have difficulty expressing their deeper thoughts and emotions with language. Instead they talk about sandwiches and oil changes. In your opinion, is Charles teaching his son to withhold his thoughts and emotions from others? Or is this type of distancing part of a larger societal role that many American men adopt to project an image of strength?

(3) Charles assumes that his own son will one day divorce. Why?

Explore

(1) Charles seems to believe that no good relationship lasts forever. Do you believe that this is true—that families, romantic couples, close friendships, and so on are all destined to fade over time and relinquish much of their goodness? If you think so, explain why human beings, in your opinion, have such difficulty maintaining strong, nurturing relationships over many years? If you think not, explain one or two strategies that might allow relationships to maintain their closeness over time.

(2) Charles's son Tommy confronts his own mortality. After viewing the skeletal remains of the La Brea Woman, he sees himself, via the mirror, as a future skeleton. In a narrative essay, explore the childhood moment when you first became aware that everyone—even you—would someday die. How did you receive this troubling news? How did it affect you?

(3) The drawings in this comic never depict a moment in which the father and son touch in any meaningful way. The father projects around him a spatial separation from other characters. Today, while in class, review whatever photos you might have of yourself—on your phone, on social media, and so on. In these photos, do you prefer to be photographed physically close to other people or do you prefer to be photographed in your own space? After reviewing these photos, write a one-page exploration in which you consider the personal meaning of the space around you. Which people do you let inside that close personal space? And which people do you tend to exclude from it?

KEVIN HUIZENGA

"Pulverize"

Kevin Huizenga grew up in a sports-oriented family; his father was a fan of fast-pitch baseball and basketball. Instead of drawing, Huizenga spent most of his early years involved in team sports. The masculine world of team sports spilled over into his high school years, when he developed an interest in drawing—superheroes in particular. With other boys at his school, he created comics that he photocopied at a local store. In college, after showing his comics to a professor, Huizenga started to take art classes. Even while a student, he published mini-comics that were distributed to comic shops. Later he created the character of Glenn Ganges, the protagonist for much of his recent work. He lives in St. Louis, where his work regularly appears in the *St. Louis Riverfront Times*.

Men and Women

IT WAS 1999 AND GLENN HAD LANDED A JOB AT REQUESTRA, A DOTCOM STARTUP.

..., AND BOB'S ON OUR SALES TEAM.

BOB BILSON.

GLENN GANGES.

EVERY NIGHT ABOUT HALF OF THE GUYS IN THE OFFICE WOULD STAY LATE AND PLAY ON THE COMPUTER NETWORK. PRETTY SOON GLENN WAS HOOKED TOO.

@#!%!

HOLY COW, THIS IS AMAZING!

HEAD SHOT

YOU HAD TO PICK A NAME AND WHAT YOUR AVATAR LOOKED LIKE. GUYS PICKED NAMES LIKE "SWEET BABY" AND "CANDYPANTS" AND "MONICA LEWINSKY."

MONICA LEWINSKY ENTERED THE GAME!

HEY SWEET BABY, CAN YOU POUR ME SOME COFFEE TOO?

?

YEAH SURE

QUITTING TIME NEVER CAME FAST ENOUGH. THEY COULDN'T WAIT TO GET "IN THERE."

SEE YOU GUYS TOMORROW.

BANG BANG BANG

THE RUSH OF COMBAT WITHOUT DANGER, MAYBE A SORE WRIST.

HEY!

DO YOU GUYS WANT TO GET PIZZA?

YEAH!

@#!% YEAH

MONICA LEWINSKY WINS THE MATCH

+45

DURING THE DAY THEY'D HAVE TO DEAL WITH CONFERENCE CALLS AND VENTURE CAPITALISTS AND PROGRAMMERS, AND IT WAS EXHAUSTING PRETENDING THAT THE DOTCOM BUZZ WASN'T REALLY B.S. – AS LONG AS THE MONEY KEPT POURING IN, OKAY...

REQUESTRA

LAMBCHOP

DARTH CAESAR

MONICA L.

BUNCHES

JERRY GARCIA

BUT AFTER 5:00 THEY DIDN'T HAVE TO WORRY ABOUT ALL THAT — JUST DODGE HARMLESS BULLETS AND AIM FOR EACH OTHER'S HEADS.

+79

16

HEAD SHOT

AAAH!

@#%!

UH OH

BZZZZ BZZZZ BZZZZ

I'M REALLY SORRY, SWEETIE, BUT WE HAVE TO WORK LATE AGAIN... YEAH I KNOW, I KNOW...

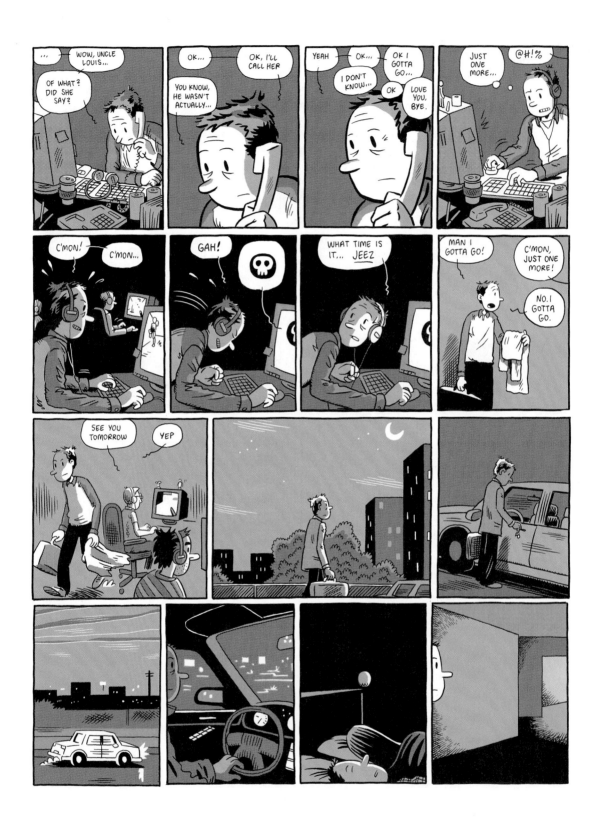

Men and Women

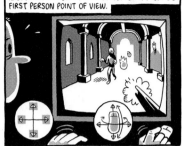

WHAT'S WEIRD IS THAT GLENN DIDN'T DREAM ABOUT PLAYING A VIDEO GAME, HE DREAMT AS IF HE HAD REALLY BEEN RUNNING THROUGH ENDLESS HALLWAYS. HIS BRAIN WAS FOOLED BY THE GAME'S FIRST PERSON POINT OF VIEW.

ALL HE SEES IS HIS GUN AND WHAT HE CAN SHOOT. ALL LOOKING IS ALSO AIMING. IT'S AN AGGRESSIVE AND PARANOID POINT OF VIEW — A PRETTY COMMON SORT OF SETUP.

THEY PLAYED DEATHMATCHES FOR HOURS, FIRST TO TWENTY, KILLS MINUS DEATHS. NOBODY AT THE OFFICE DOMINATED THE FIELD SO IT STAYED FUN.

GLENN CHASES CANDYPANTS UP TO THE ROOF, TRYING TO HIT HIM WITH THE SHOTGUN, BUT HE KEEPS DUCKING BEHIND CORNERS JUST IN TIME.

THIS MONASTERY IS THE "MAP" THEY PLAY MOST OFTEN. THE CHAPELS, ROOFTOPS, AND COURTYARDS MAKE FOR GREAT GUN BATTLES — THERE ARE A LOT OF HIDDEN PASSAGEWAYS, TRAPDOORS, ETC.

GLENN HESITATES. HE'S ALWAYS AMAZED BY THE VIEW UP HERE. ARE THOSE SUPPOSED TO BE THE HIMALAYAS?

@#!%! MONICA LEWINSKY IS UP HERE TOO!

Kevin Huizenga: "Pulverize"

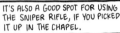

GLENN LANDS, GRABS THE ALLSLAYER, SPINS AND FIRES —

NAILING LEWINSKY MID-AIR!

THEN SUDDENLY HE'S DEAD! HEADSHOT! CANDYPANTS HAD BEEN FOLLOWING LEWINSKY AND FIRED THROUGH HIS/HER EXPLODING BODY —

MASTERFULLY PLAYED!

GLENN TURNS FROM HIS SCREEN, CURSING AND PRAISING CANDYPANTS (BOB'S NOT USUALLY THIS GOOD — HE PROBABLY JUST GOT LUCKY).

GLENN RESPAWNS IN THE CHAPEL, THEN MAKES HIS WAY THROUGH THE COURT-YARD AGAIN FOR THE BELLTOWER.

GLENN HEARS A SNIPER'S BULLET WHIZ BEHIND HIM. HE CAN SEE BOB ACROSS THE ROOM, GRINNING.

EARLIER THAT SUMMER, BOB BILSON'S MOM DIED DURING A ROUTINE SURGERY. THEN, A MONTH AGO, HIS BROTHER FELL ASLEEP ON A FLIGHT TO DETROIT AND DIDN'T WAKE UP. AN AUTOPSY FOUND A BLOOD CLOT.

SO HE'D BEEN HAVING A HELL OF A YEAR. HE MISSED SOME WORK (AND PULVERIZE).

BOB WAS USUALLY A WEAK PULVERIZE PLAYER — TOO SLOW, TOO MEEK, AN EASY KILL. YOU COULD DRIVE UP YOUR SCORE JUST HUNTING HIM. RIGHT NOW GLENN HAD 19.

AND THIS WILL BE #20, MATCH POINT.

...AND THEY WANT ME, WHEN I'M OVER THERE, TO SOMEHOW NOT ONLY DRAW THE NEW DESIGNS, BUT—

WHAT ARE YOU DOING WITH YOUR EYES?! STOP IT!!

GLENN WAS IMAGINING THAT THE TRANSPARENT, BLURRY SHAPE OF HIS NOSE IN THE LOWER CORNER OF HIS VISION WAS A ROCKET LAUNCHER.

SO I SAID, "I'M NOT GOING TO BE ABLE TO IF YOU'RE NOT—

THOUGH HE OF COURSE HAD PLAYED MANY VIOLENT VIDEO GAMES OVER THE YEARS, AND LIKE MOST BOYS EARNESTLY FANTASIZED ABOUT COMBAT SITUATIONS, GLENN'S CONSCIENCE HAD AT FIRST BEEN BOTHERED BY PULVERIZE,

HE HAD ALWAYS PREFERRED GAMES LIKE, SAY, "YIPPER YAP WORLD," CONTROLLING SCIENCE ADVENTURER GRANDMA LAGRAND AS SHE GATHERS FRUITCLUMPZ IN DEATH FOREST (YOU NEED THE MONKEY ROCKET SUIT),

AVOIDING THE ROLLER SKATING SPIDERS (BY DOUBLE ROCKET JUMPING)

IN ORDER TO THROW THE FRUIT AT A GIANT CATERPILLAR WHO HAD SPUN A COCOON IN THE ONLY SATELLITE DISH ON THE ISLAND OF SPECIAL THANKS,

WHICH HAD MESSED UP CABLE TV FOR THE NATIVE TRIBE OF RASTA-OSTRICHES,

...KEN YOU BE HELPING US, MON?...

...

IN EXCHANGE FOR WHICH THEY GIVE YOU THE MOON SALSA YOU NEED TO BRIBE THE VOLCANO WITCH TRIPLETS.

Men and Women

Men and Women

Men and Women

Men and Women

AND ... AS YOU KNOW, REVENUE HAS BEEN FALLING FOR FOUR STRAIGHT MONTHS. I'M AFRAID WE'RE GOING TO HAVE TO MAKE SOME CUTS. WE'LL BE MEETING INDIVIDUALLY WITH EACH OF YOU TOMORROW... BUT I'M OPTIMISTIC ABOUT THE FACT THAT BLAH BLAH BLAH

REMEMBER "Y2K"?

YEAH... WHAT WAS UP WITH THAT?

THAT NIGHT THEY OF COURSE WORKED PRETTY LATE, BUT AFTER STEVE WENT HOME THEY PLAYED, THOUGH SOBERLY. WHO WOULD BE LET GO? HOW MANY? WHO? MIGHT BE YOU... THEN WHAT? @#!%...

BOOM

SOME WERE OBVIOUS—EVERYBODY KNEW BOB BILSON'S FIGURES WERE THE LOWEST IN THE DEPARTMENT.

HEAD SHOT

EVERYBODY KNEW THIS WAS THE LAST NIGHT FOR CANDYPANTS.

AGAIN

WHICH MAP?

SPACE STATION

REEFL—

MONASTERY.

GLENN RESPAWNS IN THE CATACOMBS AND IMMEDIATELY HEADS FOR THE ROOF WHERE HE HAD JUST BEEN KILLED. IT'S SO FAMILIAR NOW— THE BRICKS, SHADOWS, ANGLES, AND

THE WINTRY MORNING LIGHT, WHICH NEVER CHANGES, BECAUSE THE SKY IS A JPEG. NOTHING IS EVER ADDED TO OR SUBTRACTED FROM THE ZEROES AND ONES THAT MAKE UP THE BUILDINGS OR MOUNTAINS, SO NOTHING CHANGES — TIME STANDS STILL. IT'S ALWAYS A WINTER MORNING HERE.

THEY'D SPENT MANY HOURS "IN HERE" OVER THE PAST YEAR AND A HALF, AND NOT JUST THE MONASTERY— THERE WERE MANY OTHER MAPS TO DOWNLOAD AND TRY OUT.

A TEENAGER IN DENVER HAD BUILT A WEBSITE WHERE PLAYERS COULD DOWNLOAD CUSTOM-BUILT MAPS FOR FREE. (IT WAS MORE SUCCESSFUL IN ALMOST EVERY WAY THAN REQUESTRA'S WEBSITE.)

Men and Women

ONE OF THEIR FAVORITES WAS A TROPICAL ISLAND MAP NAMED "REEFLEX" AND THEY VISIT IT AGAIN TONIGHT, THE WAVES LAPPING, GULLS CALLING OVER THE GUNFIRE. GLENN FIGHTS HIS WAY FROM THE BEACH THROUGH THE THICK, SHADOWY JUNGLE TO ONE OF THE CAVES,

WHICH LEADS TO ONE OF THE THREE ROCKY PEAKS, WHERE HE HAS A BREATHTAKING VIEW OF THE WHOLE COMPLEX, GOOD FOR SNIPING.

ANOTHER WAS "ORBITUS," A SPACE STATION HOVERING ABOVE A RED PLANET.

AS HE LEAPS FROM PLATFORM TO PLATFORM IN THE LOW GRAVITY, GLENN FEELS A DIZZY FEELING IN HIS GUT, AND LOOKING/AIMING DOWN AT THE PLANET BELOW, HE CAN SEE THE GLOW OF VOLCANIC ERUPTIONS.

"FOG OF WAR" HAD BEEN A FAVORITE FOR A FEW WEEKS. ARMED WITH ONLY SNIPER RIFLES AND CHAINSAWS, THEY WANDER A VAST SCORCHED PLAIN, SEARCHING THE HORIZON FOR EACH OTHER AND HIDING IN THE DRIFTING BANKS OF FOG.

AND NEXT WE HAVE "HALLWAYS TO HELL," WHICH IS SELF-EXPLANATORY...

ANOTHER FAVORITE MAP WAS BASED ON AN OFFICE, WITH CUBICLES AND FAX MACHINES AND A BREAK ROOM AND EVERYTHING,

ONLY THE PLAYERS ARE SHRUNK TO THE SIZE OF MICE. THE CUBICLES ARE LIKE CANYONS, AND OF COURSE PULVERIZE IS ON EVERY SCREEN...

Men and Women

THAT WAS WEIRD, SEEING BOB BILSON EARLIER TODAY.*

I WONDER HOW HE'S DOING.

* SEE GANGES #1, "THE LITTERER"

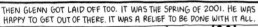

THEN GLENN GOT LAID OFF TOO. IT WAS THE SPRING OF 2001. HE WAS HAPPY TO GET OUT OF THERE. IT WAS A RELIEF TO BE DONE WITH IT ALL.

WE JUST COULDN'T HAVE FORESEEN THE DOWNTURN IN THE ECONOMY AND SO—

REQUESTRA FOLDED LESS THAN A YEAR LATER. STEVE STANE WENT TO WORK ON HIS FATHER'S CAMPAIGN, AND IN 2003, WOULD BE BRIEFLY IN CHARGE OF RESTARTING THE IRAQI STOCK MARKET.

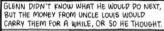

GLENN DIDN'T KNOW WHAT HE WOULD DO NEXT, BUT THE MONEY FROM UNCLE LOUIS WOULD CARRY THEM FOR A WHILE, OR SO HE THOUGHT.

HE COULD HAVE PLAYED PULVERIZE OVER THE INTERNET AT HOME, BUT WENDY BLEW HER TOP WHEN HE CONFESSED TO WHAT HE'D BEEN DOING ALL THOSE LATE NIGHTS.

@#!%

OH WELL,

I GUESS I'LL GO BACK TO BED, TRY TO GET SOME SLEEP...

I SHOULDN'T HAVE DRUNK ALL THAT COFFEE!

AND BESIDES, IT WOULDN'T BE THE SAME. EVEN STILL, SOMETIMES GLENN GETS A POWERFUL LONGING

TO GO BACK

AND PLAY THAT GAME AGAIN

WITH THOSE GUYS—

GET THE SNIPER RIFLE, ZOOM IN...

JUST ONE MORE...

Men and Women

Analyze

(1) In your opinion, is Glenn's interest in Pulverize an "addiction"—that is, an obsession that he may not fully control? If so, explain why extended video play may create an experience that some users have trouble leaving.

(2) Glenn lies to Wendy; he doesn't focus fully on his work; he appears to be involved more with his coworkers in virtual space than in his actual life. Do you find him a sympathetic or likeable character? If so, why?

(3) In your opinion, who is more responsible for the failure of Requestra—common employees like Glenn who do not focus their attentions fully on their job or executives like Steve who build a poor public and marketing image for the company: "We don't know [the future of Internet business]. And that's a good thing"?

(4) In the late 1990s and early 2000s (when "Pulverize" is set), the Internet was transforming how people communicated, did business, and even presented themselves. As you consider present-day culture, what new technologies will change the way people live in the next ten years?

Explore

(1) Glenn justifies his obsession with Pulverize by rationalizing that he wasn't shooting at people—or even representations of people—but rather he was "just shooting dots at dots." Do you believe there is a meaningful difference between triangular spaceships shooting "dots" in very early video games and realistic computer-generated images of people shooting bullets and missiles in more sophisticated video games?

(2) Glenn is so involved with the video game Pulverize that it changes how he views the world around him. With other members of your class, develop a list of beneficial and potentially harmful effects of spending so much time in a virtual environment.

(3) The comic depicts the combat-related, first-person-shooter video game as part of masculine culture—with all of the players young men, even though the company employs young women. Discuss cultural concepts of masculinity and femininity, with an eye toward explaining the author's presentation of video culture here as belonging primarily to young men. What are current cultural concepts of masculinity and femininity? How do they relate to the gender separation depicted in this comic?

(4) In an essay, define the central concept of masculinity or femininity in your family. What did it mean to be a girl or a boy in the house where you grew up? Were there any differences in the expectations for and treatment of boys compared to that of girls? How did these early ideas about gender help create the person you are now?

Young Adulthood

The young adult experience has long been a centerpiece concern of American literature, from Mark Twain's *The Adventures of Huckleberry Finn* (1884) to Maureen Daley's *Seventeenth Summer* (1942) and J. D. Salinger's *The Catcher in the Rye* (1951). It is, therefore, no wonder that graphic novels similarly feature young protagonists. These characters, filled with yearnings and insecurities, explore what it means to grow up in a world where one doesn't always seem to fit. In Alison Bechdel's graphic memoir *Fun Home*, the young narrator struggles to understand herself in a family filled with secrets. The protagonist of "Blue Note" is confronted with the belief that the ultimate meaning of life may be wholly personal, that "there's no ultimate truth, just shifting sets of perceptions, all of which are equally true."

The worlds captured in these selections focus on the uncomfortable middle ground between childhood and adult experience, that strange murky space of high school, college, and first jobs. These years, for many people, represent the most turbulent and dramatic period of life, the shaking off of childhood beliefs and the journey into adult responsibilities. For some, the twilight of youth represents strong sensations—a heightened sense of experience—that haunts them for the rest of their lives. The lead character in "Dance with the Ventures" lives alone, in an empty apartment, but aches so strongly for the music of his youth that he spends his morning sorting through old records that other tenants leave by the curb as trash. Derf's music-inspired "The Bank" also explores the youth music scene, focusing on the punk rock scene in Akron, Ohio. In an interview with www.newsrama.com, Derf explains how the punk rock music scene "all revolved around this great club, The Bank, which was just that: an abandoned bank . . . It was this incredible metaphor for what was going on in Akron, the boom town gone bust, and a bank, a symbol of American capitalism, now home to this nihilistic caterwaul."

The readings in this chapter invite us to explore the daunting, exciting, and sometimes threatening new situations and challenges that young people encounter as they maneuver toward adulthood. Rebellion. Identity. Maturity. Community. Conformity. Security. Family. Personal responsibility. Taken together, this grouping reveals how the experience of the struggling outsider is far closer to the norm than one might expect.

ALISON BECHDEL

Fun Home: A Family Tragicomic

Early in her career, Alison Bechdel was widely known for her comic strip, *Dykes to Watch Out For*, which premiered in 1983 and ran for nearly two decades in alt-weekly newspapers. *Fun Home*, a graphic memoir, was her first published book, a *New York Times* bestseller, and also one of the *Times*'s "10 Best Books of the Year." Her work draws largely on her own experience, often exploring family through memory. Her work frequently investigates the space between mainstream social roles and personal desires, between oppression and freedom. Recently, Bechdel has continued her autobiography exploration of these themes in a new graphic memoir, *Are You My Mother?*

LIKE MANY FATHERS, MINE COULD OCCASIONALLY BE PREVAILED ON FOR A SPOT OF "AIRPLANE."

AS HE LAUNCHED ME, MY FULL WEIGHT WOULD FALL ON THE PIVOT POINT BETWEEN HIS FEET AND MY STOMACH.

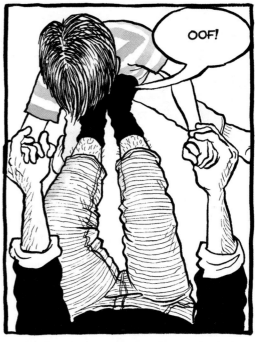

IT WAS A DISCOMFORT WELL WORTH THE RARE PHYSICAL CONTACT, AND CERTAINLY WORTH THE MOMENT OF PERFECT BALANCE WHEN I SOARED ABOVE HIM.

IN THE CIRCUS, ACROBATICS WHERE ONE PERSON LIES ON THE FLOOR BALANCING ANOTHER ARE CALLED "ICARIAN GAMES."

CONSIDERING THE FATE OF ICARUS AFTER HE FLOUTED HIS FATHER'S ADVICE AND FLEW SO CLOSE TO THE SUN HIS WINGS MELTED, PERHAPS SOME DARK HUMOR IS INTENDED.

BUT BEFORE HE DID SO, HE MANAGED TO GET QUITE A LOT DONE.

HIS GREATEST ACHIEVEMENT, ARGUABLY, WAS HIS MONOMANIACAL RESTORATION OF OUR OLD HOUSE.

Young Adulthood

WHEN OTHER CHILDREN CALLED OUR HOUSE A MANSION, I WOULD DEMUR. I RESENTED THE IMPLICATION THAT MY FAMILY WAS RICH, OR UNUSUAL IN ANY WAY.

IN FACT, WE WERE UNUSUAL, THOUGH I WOULDN'T APPRECIATE EXACTLY HOW UNUSUAL UNTIL MUCH LATER. BUT WE WERE NOT RICH.

IT'S JUST A HOUSE.

ALISON!

WHAT?

SEND TAMMI HOME. YOU HAVE WORK TO DO.

THE GILT CORNICES, THE MARBLE FIREPLACE, THE CRYSTAL CHANDELIERS, THE SHELVES OF CALF-BOUND BOOKS--THESE WERE NOT SO MUCH BOUGHT AS PRODUCED FROM THIN AIR BY MY FATHER'S REMARKABLE LEGERDEMAIN.

WASH THESE OLD CURTAINS SO WE CAN PUT UP THE HAND-EMBROIDERED LACE ONES I FOUND IN MRS. STRUMP'S ATTIC.

MY FATHER COULD SPIN GARBAGE...

...INTO GOLD.

HE COULD TRANSFIGURE A ROOM WITH THE SMALLEST OFFHAND FLOURISH.

HE COULD CONJURE AN ENTIRE, FINISHED PERIOD INTERIOR FROM A PAINT CHIP.

HE WAS AN ALCHEMIST OF APPEARANCE, A SAVANT OF SURFACE, A DAEDALUS OF DECOR.

FOR IF MY FATHER WAS ICARUS, HE WAS ALSO DAEDALUS--THAT SKILLFUL ARTIFICER, THAT MAD SCIENTIST WHO BUILT THE WINGS FOR HIS SON AND DESIGNED THE FAMOUS LABYRINTH...

THIS IS THE WALLPAPER FOR MY ROOM?

...AND WHO ANSWERED NOT TO THE LAWS OF SOCIETY, BUT TO THOSE OF HIS CRAFT.

BUT I **HATE** PINK! I **HATE** FLOWERS!

TOUGH TITTY.

HISTORICAL RESTORATION WASN'T HIS JOB.

(TWELFTH-GRADE ENGLISH)

ARCHI-TECTURAL DIGEST

IT WAS HIS PASSION. AND I MEAN PASSION IN EVERY SENSE OF THE WORD.

LIBIDINAL. MANIC. MARTYRED.

OUR GOTHIC REVIVAL HOUSE HAD BEEN BUILT DURING THE SMALL PENNSYLVANIA TOWN'S ONE BRIEF MOMENT OF WEALTH, FROM THE LUMBER INDUSTRY, IN 1867.

BUT LOCAL FORTUNES HAD DECLINED STEADILY FROM THAT POINT, AND WHEN MY PARENTS BOUGHT THE PLACE IN 1962, IT WAS A SHELL OF ITS FORMER SELF.

THE SHUTTERS AND SCROLLWORK WERE GONE. THE CLAPBOARDS HAD BEEN SHEATHED WITH SCABROUS SHINGLES.

Young Adulthood

THE BARE LIGHTBULBS REVEALED DINGY WARTIME WALLPAPER AND WOODWORK PAINTED PASTEL GREEN.

ALL THAT WAS LEFT OF THE HOUSE'S LUMBER-ERA GLORY WERE THE EXUBERANT FRONT PORCH SUPPORTS.

BUT OVER THE NEXT EIGHTEEN YEARS, MY FATHER WOULD RESTORE THE HOUSE TO ITS ORIGINAL CONDITION, AND THEN SOME.

JESUS! THIS MUST BE THE PATTERN FOR THE ORIGINAL BARGEBOARD!

HE WOULD PERFORM, AS DAEDALUS DID, DAZZLING DISPLAYS OF ARTFULNESS.

HE WOULD CULTIVATE THE BARREN YARD... ...INTO A LUSH, FLOWERING LANDSCAPE.

HE WOULD MANIPULATE FLAGSTONES THAT WEIGHED HALF A TON... ...AND THE THINNEST, QUIVERING LAYERS OF GOLD LEAF.

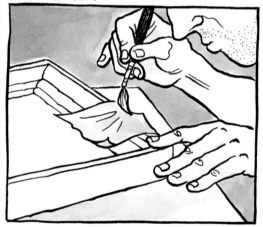

IT COULD HAVE BEEN A ROMANTIC STORY, LIKE IN *IT'S A WONDERFUL LIFE,* WHEN JIMMY STEWART AND DONNA REED FIX UP THAT BIG OLD HOUSE AND RAISE THEIR FAMILY THERE.

Young Adulthood

BUT IN THE MOVIE WHEN JIMMY STEWART COMES HOME ONE NIGHT AND STARTS YELLING AT EVERYONE...

...IT'S OUT OF THE ORDINARY.

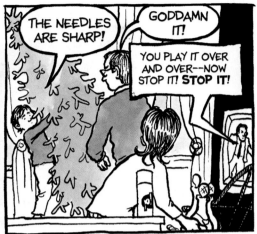

DAEDALUS, TOO, WAS INDIFFERENT TO THE HUMAN COST OF HIS PROJECTS.

HE BLITHELY BETRAYED THE KING, FOR EXAMPLE, WHEN THE QUEEN ASKED HIM TO BUILD HER A COW DISGUISE SO SHE COULD SEDUCE THE WHITE BULL.

INDEED, THE RESULT OF THAT SCHEME—A HALF-BULL, HALF-MAN MONSTER—INSPIRED DAEDALUS'S GREATEST CREATION YET.

HE HID THE MINOTAUR IN THE LABYRINTH—A MAZE OF PASSAGES AND ROOMS OPENING ENDLESSLY INTO ONE ANOTHER...

...AND FROM WHICH, AS STRAY YOUTHS AND MAIDENS DISCOVERED TO THEIR PERIL...

...ESCAPE WAS IMPOSSIBLE.

THEN THERE ARE THOSE FAMOUS WINGS. WAS DAEDALUS REALLY STRICKEN WITH GRIEF WHEN ICARUS FELL INTO THE SEA?

OR JUST DISAPPOINTED BY THE DESIGN FAILURE?

Young Adulthood

SOMETIMES, WHEN THINGS WERE GOING WELL, I THINK MY FATHER ACTUALLY ENJOYED HAVING A FAMILY.

AND OF COURSE, MY BROTHERS AND I WERE FREE LABOR. DAD CONSIDERED US EXTENSIONS OF HIS OWN BODY, LIKE PRECISION ROBOT ARMS.

OR AT LEAST, THE AIR OF AUTHENTICITY WE LENT TO HIS EXHIBIT. A SORT OF STILL LIFE WITH CHILDREN.

PUT HOT, SOAPY WATER IN THE SINK AND GET SOME CLEAN RAGS.

IN THIS REGARD, IT WAS LIKE BEING RAISED NOT BY JIMMY BUT BY MARTHA STEWART.

IN THEORY, HIS ARRANGEMENT WITH MY MOTHER WAS MORE COOPERATIVE.

IN PRACTICE, IT WAS NOT.

WHAT DO YOU THINK OF THIS GAS CHANDELIER?

BORDELLO.

AUCTION CATALOG

WE EACH RESISTED IN OUR OWN WAYS, BUT IN THE END WE WERE EQUALLY POWERLESS BEFORE MY FATHER'S CURATORIAL ONSLAUGHT.

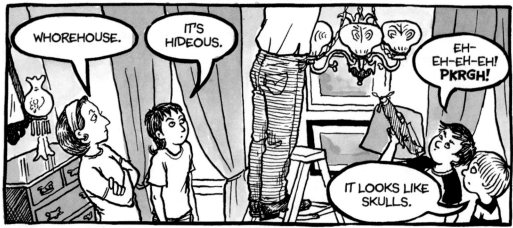

MY BROTHERS AND I COULDN'T COMPETE WITH THE ASTRAL LAMPS AND GIRANDOLES AND HEPPLEWHITE SUITE CHAIRS. THEY WERE PERFECT.

I GREW TO RESENT THE WAY MY FATHER TREATED HIS FURNITURE LIKE CHILDREN, AND HIS CHILDREN LIKE FURNITURE.

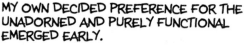

MY OWN DECIDED PREFERENCE FOR THE UNADORNED AND PURELY FUNCTIONAL EMERGED EARLY.

I WAS SPARTAN TO MY FATHER'S ATHENIAN.

MODERN TO HIS VICTORIAN.

BUTCH TO HIS NELLY.

UTILITARIAN TO HIS AESTHETE.

I DEVELOPED A CONTEMPT FOR USE-
LESS ORNAMENT. WHAT FUNCTION WAS
SERVED BY THE SCROLLS, TASSELS, AND
BRIC-A-BRAC THAT INFESTED OUR HOUSE?

IF ANYTHING, THEY OBSCURED FUNCTION.
THEY WERE EMBELLISHMENTS IN THE
WORST SENSE.

PLING
KLINK

THEY WERE LIES.

INCIPIENT
YELLOW
LUNG
DISEASE

MY FATHER BEGAN TO SEEM MORALLY
SUSPECT TO ME LONG BEFORE I KNEW
THAT HE ACTUALLY HAD A DARK SECRET.

MOM SAYS
HURRY UP.

"BRONZING
STICK"

HE USED HIS SKILLFUL ARTIFICE NOT TO MAKE THINGS, BUT TO MAKE THINGS APPEAR
TO BE WHAT THEY WERE NOT.

MASS WILL BE
OVER BEFORE WE
GET THERE.

THAT IS TO SAY,
IMPECCABLE.

Young Adulthood

HE APPEARED TO BE AN IDEAL HUSBAND AND FATHER, FOR EXAMPLE.

IT'S TEMPTING TO SUGGEST, IN RETRO-SPECT, THAT OUR FAMILY WAS A SHAM.

THAT OUR HOUSE WAS NOT A REAL HOME AT ALL BUT THE SIMULACRUM OF ONE, A MUSEUM.

YET WE REALLY WERE A FAMILY, AND WE REALLY DID LIVE IN THOSE PERIOD ROOMS.

STILL, SOMETHING VITAL WAS MISSING.

AN ELASTICITY, A MARGIN FOR ERROR.

MOST PEOPLE, I IMAGINE, LEARN TO ACCEPT THAT THEY'RE NOT PERFECT.

BUT AN IDLE REMARK ABOUT MY FATHER'S TIE OVER BREAKFAST COULD SEND HIM INTO A TAILSPIN.

DON'T CHANGE IT! WE'RE LATE!

ALSO AN ENGLISH TEACHER

MY MOTHER ESTABLISHED A RULE.

NO COMMENTS ON HIS APPEARANCE. IS THAT UNDERSTOOD?

WHAT IF IT'S SOMETHING GOOD?

GOOD, BAD, IT DOESN'T MATTER.

IF WE COULDN'T CRITICIZE MY FATHER, SHOWING AFFECTION FOR HIM WAS AN EVEN DICIER VENTURE.

THE Stones of VENICE RUSKIN

WE WERE NOT A PHYSICALLY EXPRESSIVE FAMILY, TO SAY THE LEAST. BUT ONCE I WAS UNACCOUNTABLY MOVED TO KISS MY FATHER GOOD NIGHT.

HAVING LITTLE PRACTICE WITH THE GES-TURE, ALL I MANAGED WAS TO GRAB HIS HAND AND BUSS THE KNUCKLES LIGHTLY...

...AS IF HE WERE A BISHOP OR AN ELEGANT LADY, BEFORE RUSHING FROM THE ROOM IN EMBARRASSMENT.

THIS EMBARRASSMENT ON MY PART WAS A TINY SCALE MODEL OF MY FATHER'S MORE FULLY DEVELOPED SELF-LOATHING.

HIS SHAME INHABITED OUR HOUSE AS PERVASIVELY AND INVISIBLY AS THE AROMATIC MUSK OF AGING MAHOGANY.

IN FACT, THE METICULOUS, PERIOD INTERIORS WERE EXPRESSLY DESIGNED TO CONCEAL IT.

MIRRORS, DISTRACTING BRONZES, MULTIPLE DOORWAYS. VISITORS OFTEN GOT LOST UPSTAIRS.

GRACIOUS, I ALMOST WALKED RIGHT INTO THIS!

Young Adulthood

MY MOTHER, MY BROTHERS, AND I KNEW OUR WAY AROUND WELL ENOUGH, BUT IT WAS IMPOSSIBLE TO TELL IF THE MINOTAUR LAY BEYOND THE NEXT CORNER.

AND THE CONSTANT TENSION WAS HEIGHTENED BY THE FACT THAT SOME ENCOUNTERS COULD BE QUITE PLEASANT.

HIS BURSTS OF KINDNESS WERE AS INCANDESCENT AS HIS TANTRUMS WERE DARK.

ALTHOUGH I'M GOOD AT ENUMERATING MY FATHER'S FLAWS, IT'S HARD FOR ME TO SUSTAIN MUCH ANGER AT HIM.

I EXPECT THIS IS PARTLY BECAUSE HE'S DEAD, AND PARTLY BECAUSE THE BAR IS LOWER FOR FATHERS THAN FOR MOTHERS.

STOP SPLASHING!

IN MY EYES!

HOLD STILL, DAMMIT!

MY MOTHER MUST HAVE BATHED ME HUNDREDS OF TIMES. BUT IT'S MY FATHER RINSING ME OFF WITH THE PURPLE METAL CUP THAT I REMEMBER MOST CLEARLY.

THE SUFFUSION OF WARMTH AS THE HOT WATER SLUICED OVER ME...

...THE SUDDEN, UNBEARABLE COLD OF ITS ABSENCE.

AGAIN!

WAS HE A GOOD FATHER? I WANT TO SAY, "AT LEAST HE STUCK AROUND." BUT OF COURSE, HE DIDN'T.

Young Adulthood

IT'S TRUE THAT HE DIDN'T KILL HIMSELF UNTIL I WAS NEARLY TWENTY.

BUT HIS ABSENCE RESONATED RETRO-ACTIVELY, ECHOING BACK THROUGH ALL THE TIME I KNEW HIM.

MAYBE IT WAS THE CONVERSE OF THE WAY AMPUTEES FEEL PAIN IN A MISSING LIMB.

HE REALLY WAS THERE ALL THOSE YEARS, A FLESH-AND-BLOOD PRESENCE STEAMING OFF THE WALLPAPER, DIGGING UP THE DOGWOODS, POLISHING THE FINIALS...

...SMELLING OF SAWDUST AND SWEAT AND DESIGNER COLOGNE.

BUT I ACHED AS IF HE WERE ALREADY GONE.

Analyze

(1) The initial defining image in *Fun Home* is an image of Alison Bechdel flying above her father in a game of airplane. Both the image and the text draw our attention to the space between them. In your own words, how would you describe that space? What areas connect them?

(2) Ironically, the father in *Fun Home* devotes himself to restoration of the family home, but not to the improvement of his family. In what ways do you feel that the father is responsible for problems in the family? The narration also claims that the father "could spin garbage into gold." With this in mind, do you see any ways in which the father contributes to his family's well-being?

(3) The narration defines Alison and her father as fundamentally different: "I was Spartan to my father's Athenian, Modern to his Victorian." In terms of their personalities, do you see them as primarily different or as strikingly similar?

(4) Do you believe that the overarching emotion that Alison has for her father is closer to love or to resentment?

Explore

(1) *Fun Home* repeatedly calls attention to works of myth, particularly the stories Daedalus and the Minotaur and Daedalus and Icarus. Explore ways in which these myths and the story of *Fun Home* speak to and resonate with each other.

(2) Alison suggests that her family was, at times, a simulacrum of a family—with their roles defined by film, social expectation and even religion. In what ways does Alison contribute—perhaps unwittingly—to the artificiality of her family life?

(3) In places, Alison longs for an idealized family, as represented in film (*It's a Wonderful Life*). Review the film *It's a Wonderful Life*. In your opinion, which offers a more authentic and meaningful exploration of family life and community: *Fun Home* or *It's a Wonderful Life*?

(4) Review the drawings of the father and Alison. What emotions frame the appearance of each figure?

GABRIELLE BELL

"Amy Was a Babysitter"

Gabrielle Bell was born in England, but at the age of two, she moved to northern California with her mother. She attended Humboldt State University and City College of San Francisco, where she studied art. In 1998 she began to self-publish her comics in yearly collections. Her art fluctuates between surrealism and realist line drawings. More so than most contemporary comic artists, her understanding of narrative is strongly related to the traditions of the American short story. As such, our textbook includes more than one entry by Gabrielle Bell. Presently she lives in Brooklyn, New York.

Amy was a babysitter. In her small town where she'd grown up, she prided herself on being well-known and trusted.

Both responsible and popular with the children, she was welcome in any home.

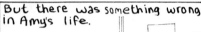

But there was something wrong in Amy's life.

She was dissatisfied. At nineteen, she was both cynical and full of irrational dreams.

She was discontented, but she devoted everything to the children, and never so much as grew impatient with them.

The one thing that distinguished her most as a great babysitter was her ability to captivate anyone around with her imaginative stories.

Secretly, she saved up her money, and planned a trip to the city.

But she was relied on by both parents and children; and life without her could not be imagined.

...AND IN THIS TOWN THERE WERE NO DOORBELLS SO YOU HAD TO SHOUT UP AT THE WINDOWS OR THROW LITTLE STONES, AND IT WAS CUSTOMARY, UPON ENTERING SOMEONE'S HOUSE, TO TELL YOUR HOST A SECRET YOU'VE NEVER TOLD BEFORE...

It seemed to her that there was a conspiracy to keep her home forever.

AMY! WHAT ARE YOU DOING?

I'M LEAVING TOWN. I CAN'T STAND ANOTHER SECOND HERE.

CAN I JUST GET YOU TO STAY WITH JAMIE FOR A COUPLE HOURS, AND THEN WE CAN ALL GO OUT FOR PIZZA...?

PIZZA?

SAY YES SAY YES SAY YES SAY YES SAY YES

She was a very melodramatic girl.

AND THEN, ONE DAY, AFTER YEARS OF PRACTICE, SHE FINALLY TAUGHT HERSELF TO FLY. IT CAME AS NATURALLY TO HER AS BREATHING; AND AS SHE DARTED UP TO THE CLOUDS, SHE FOUND THAT ALL OF HER WORRIES WERE TOO HEAVY TO COME WITH HER, SO THEY DROPPED DOWN TO THE EARTH WITH A THUD...

So, on one sad day she got up the courage to leave; and all the children cried.

NOW, REMEMBER WHAT I TOLD YOU ABOUT LONG DIVISION...

GATE 3

On the bus she experienced the lonliest time of her life.

She found herself a cheap, cozy little studio. She would have been excited but she was too miserable and scared.

She tried to get a job but she didn't know how to act at the interviews.

SO, AMY, TELL ME, HOW CAN WE APPLY YOUR SKILLS AS A BABYSITTER TO OUR COMPANY?

She spent a lot of time at the bookstore.

EXCUSE ME BUT IF YOUR GOING TO READ THAT WHOLE THING YOU'LL HAVE TO BUY IT.

Because of her excellent references, she managed to find a babysitting job, but t city kids found her weird.

NO I DON'T WANT TO HEAR NO STORY.

AND IF YOU TRY AN' MAKE ME GO TO BED, BITCH, I'll TELL MY PARENTS YOU DID DIRTY THINGS TO ME.

She read constanty, often a book a day.

The city frightened her. Soon she was only leaving her house to go to the market or the bookstore.

When she was down to her last hundred dollars, she bought herself a bus ticket home, and took herself out to dinner.

AND A CARAFE OF HOUSE RED!

ALL RIGHT... CAN I SEE YOUR I.D. PLEASE?

MY I.D? HA HA! OH YOU FLATTER ME!

She would be needing a job as soon as she got home.

AMY!!!

She dreaded the time she would be asked;

SO; HOW WAS YOUR TRIP?

THE EMPIRE STRIKES

So she made something up.

WELL I MET THESE GIRLS ON THE BUS AND WE GOT KICKED OFF IN SOME NO-WHERE TOWN SO WE ENDED UP HITCHHIKING DOWN TO TEXAS WHERE WE STARTED A BAND, WHICH WAS COOL UNTIL ONE OF THE GIRLS GOT PREGNANT...

And they wanted to hear more; so she kept making things up, until she began to believe them herself.

IN ISTANBUL I MET THIS FORTUNE TELLER WHO WAS TRYING TO KILL ME BECAUSE SHE KNEW HER HUSBAND WAS DESTINED TO FALL IN LOVE WITH ME...

She spoke so much of her imagined adventures that she soon thought of herself as a world traveller.

NEVER, IN ALL MY TRAVELS HAVE I EVER TASTED A COOKIE THIS DELECTABLE!

She was a strange girl, but with children she could always be trusted.

IN CHINA THERE'S A TOWN WHERE THEY'VE PROGRAMMED ROBOTS TO DO ALL THE CHORES LIKE THE FARMING AND COOKING AND CLEANING SO THE PEOPLE DEVOTE THEIR TIME TO MAK-ING WIND CHIMES AND BELLS AND DRUMS AND YOU CAN HEAR IT FOR MILES AROUND

And through the years her fame spread, and wealthy parents brought their kids from miles around, and she charged ridiculously large sums of money.

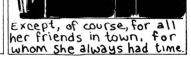

AMY'S BABYSITTING SERVICE NEXT EX

MAIN STR NEXT ST

Except, of course, for all her friends in town, for whom she always had time.

Analyze

(1) Amy works in a low-paying job (babysitting), yet she finds other rewards in her work beyond money. In your opinion, is this a reasonable way for a young person to think about employment?

(2) Amy lies, acts antisocial, makes disparaging statements about math, and has no idea how to interview for a job, yet parents feel she is trustworthy with their children. Why?

(3) Why does Amy lie about her experience in "the city"? In your opinion, are these lies morally justifiable because they entertain children and eventually allow Amy to earn a good living as a babysitter?

(4) Amy is unable to realize her dream of living and working in the city (beyond her brief stay there), yet she eventually grows her babysitting business. In your opinion, is Amy a success or a failure?

Explore

(1) In the comic, Amy believes that certain school subjects are valuable and others are not. For example, she believes reading is valuable but long division "rots your brain and has no relevance to real life." Make a list of five school subjects that have the most relevance to your life. In your opinion, what qualities should a formal education impart to students: job training (such as engineering and business), personal enrichment (such as the arts and literature), skills of citizenship (such as political science and cultural studies), values and ethics (such as philosophy and law), and general skills and knowledge (such as introductory biology and algebra)?

(2) Amy moves from a small town to the city. After high school, many students move from their hometown to a college town—or at the very least from a high school campus to a collegiate one. Make a list of the most noticeable cultural differences between your experience in high school and your experience in college.

(3) Using only the drawings of Amy (and ignoring the verbal narration and dialogue), describe Amy's emotions in the three sections of her story: at home, in the city, and returning home. How is emotion conveyed through gesture and facial expression?

(4) Write an essay about an experience in which you worked a low-paying job. What did you learn from the experience? Aside from a paycheck, what skills did you develop through your employment?

LYNDA BARRY

"San Francisco"

Born in 1956, Linda Jean Barry grew up in rural Wisconsin, where her father was a meat-cutter and her mother a hospital housekeeper. When she was twelve years old, her parents divorced. That same year she changed the spelling of her first name: from Linda to Lynda. In junior high, she grew attracted to erratic drawings of R. Crumb. At the age of twenty-three, Barry became a full-time artist when her quirky, sardonic strip *Ernie Pook's Comeek* was syndicated in alternative weekly newspapers across the country.

BARRY

TOWARD the END OF each AUGUST THE "BACK-TO-SCHOOL" ADS BEGIN to APPEAR and THOUGH I AM well PAST SCHOOL age, THEY NEVER FAIL to GIVE ME A certain FEELING, a curious MIX OF ANXIETY, Dread AND excitement.

OH MAN!

ALREADY?

BACK TO SCHOOL SALE!

SCHOOL ALWAYS brought NEW things INTO MY LIFE, NEW PEOPLE, NEW ideas, NEW hope ABOUT NOT being SUCH A WEIRDO, ABOUT having a MIRACLE HAPPEN that WOULD GIVE me STRAIGHT A's, straight HAIR, and a SUPER POPULAR YEAR.

LORD, PLEASE KEEP ME FROM HAVING TO GET HORRIBLE SHOES AGAIN THIS YEAR.

PLEASE KEEP MOM AWAY FROM SEAR'S JUNIOR BOOT SHOP.

Back to School SALE

BUT it ALSO MEANT the END OF Summer. NO MATTER IF the HOT, PRETTY DAYS continued, once SCHOOL STARTED, SUMMER WAS over, AND WHOEVER I HAD been ALL that YEAR WAS over too. THE 6TH GRADER DIES. THE 7th grader IS BORN.

13, 14, 15....

WHOA.

16 MORE DAYS, MAN.

MUTUAL FISH COMPANY

AUGUST

'TIL WHAT? 'TIL YOU REALIZE YOU'RE ACTUALLY AN IDIOT?

That SUMMER, the one BEFORE 7th GRADE BEGAN, I DISCOVERED THE radio. IT HAD ALWAYS been there, BUT THAT Summer IT STARTED TELLING ME THINGS, it WHISPERED to me ABOUT a WORLD OUT THERE, GAVE me CLUES in SONGS, GAVE numbers TO CALL, GAVE ME FEELINGS I COULDN'T resist.

BE THE FIFTH CALLER AND WIN TICKETS TO SEE THE TROGGS LIVE!

C'MON! ANSWER! C'MON, MAN!

At NIGHT, ESPECIALLY, IN the PITCH DARK of MY BASEMENT BED-room, the SONGS were POWERFUL, THE D.J. SEEMED TO be PLAYING MY FUTURE of fantastic MAGICAL encounters WITH PEOPLE WHO WOULD LEAD ME to SOMETHING I DIDN'T HAVE a name FOR YET.

♪ WHEN YOU'VE MADE YOUR MIND UP FOREVER TO BE MINE ♪ I'LL PICK UP YOUR HAND ♪ AND SLOWLY BLOW YOUR LITTLE MIND ♪

OF course THERE WOULD be A GUY. A cute GUY, POSSIBLY a HIPPIE, POSSIBLY he'd HAVE A GUITAR, and HE'D FREAK out WHEN HE saw ME because our LOVE WOULD BE SO REAL. In THE darkness SUCH VISIONS OF MY FUTURE BLOOMED.

OH DONOVAN, I LOVE YOU TOO. BUT MY MOM HATES HIPPIES.

RUN AWAY WITH YOU? OH DONOVAN. PLEASE DON'T MAKE ME CHOOSE

DURING the DAY I WAS still A KID. I HUNG around THE USUAL PEOPLE, PLAYED the USUAL KICK-BALL GAME, Drank THE USUAL GREEN KOOL-AID AND waited FOR the ICE CREAM man.

(MY BEST FRIEND. SHE WAS 2 YEARS YOUNGER)

YOU GONNA DO LIKE SHONITA AND THEM WHEN YOU START 7th GRADE?

DO LIKE WHAT?

GET WEIRD TO PEOPLE.

LIKE HOW?

LIKE HOW THEY DON'T PLAY NOTHING AND THEY ALWAYS KEEP GOING OTHER PLACES.

MY BEST FRIEND GLADYS was about TO START 5th GRADE. SHE WAS a VERY cool PERSON and OUR AGE DIFFERENCE never mattered TO ME BEFORE. BUT DURING THOSE last WEEKS OF summer I WAS STARTING to FEEL SICK ABOUT it.

(SHE WAS TINY FOR HER AGE)

YOU GONNA DO LIKE THAT? GET ALL TEENAGERISH?

ARE YA?

YA GONNA QUIT HANGING AROUND WITH ME?

Young Adulthood

That SAME DAY FIVE *hippies* CAME DOWN OUR STREET. THEY *must* HAVE BEEN *lost*. NO HIPPIES HAD *ever* COME DOWN *our* STREET BEFORE.

UH-OH. LOOK.

IT'S THEM.

I WANTED TO FOLLOW *them*. GLADYS DIDN'T. The HIPPIES TURNED *the* CORNER AND *were* GONE. GLADYS *stared* AT ME *and* I STARED BACK. *She* STARTED TO SAY SOMETHING *but* I GOT UP *and* RAN.

DON'T WAIT UP, GLADYS!

TRAITOR! YA STUPID IDIOT TRAITOR!

GLADYS *was* THE ONLY *one* WHO *knew* I WANTED *to* BE A HIPPIE *I* TALKED *about* SAN FRANCISCO. *There* WAS A SONG ABOUT IT *that* PLAYED ON THE RADIO. IT *had* A *sad*, BEAUTIFUL MELODY. *I* SANG IT FOR GLADYS. I *didn't* KNOW WHY *she* SEEMED TO *hate* IT. I THOUGHT *she* WAS JUST TOO YOUNG.

YA UGLY, STUPID TRAITOR!

RUN!

GO 'HEAD!

RUN!

BUT SHE *knew* BEFORE *I did* THAT *I* WAS ABOUT *to* LEAVE *and* NEVER *come* BACK. SAN FRANCISCO. SOMETHING *like* SAN FRANCISCO WAS EXPANDING *inside* OF ME AND *I* DIDN'T WANT IT *to* STOP. I WATCHED *the* HIPPIES GET ON *the* NUMBER SEVEN BUS *and* RIDE AWAY.

BUS STOP

TAKE ME.

TAKE ME WITH YOU.

The LAST DAYS OF *summer* ARE ALWAYS SO SAD. FLOWERS *lose* THEIR PETALS *and* BECOME HARD SEEDS. *I* TOOK THE NUMBER SEVEN BUS *in* SEARCH OF THE HIPPIES. *I* AVOIDED GLADYS.

I LISTENED *to* THE RADIO FOR LOCATIONS AND CHANGED *buses downtown* LOOKING *out* THE WINDOW FOR "THE HAPPENING," *the* PLACE WHERE *the* HIPPIES ALL GROOVED *in* THE *sun. I knew* IT WAS OUT THERE. ALL I NEEDED *was* TO FIND *the* RIGHT *bus.*

END OF THE LINE, SWEETHEART. YOU HAVE TO GET OFF.

WHAT DO YOU MEAN?

I DON'T GO NO FURTHER.

BUT WHERE'S THE HIPPIES?

Please don't disturb driver.

YOU RIDE THE #27? EVERYDAY.

YOU EVER SEE WILD LOOKING PEOPLE ACTING MAGICAL WITH STICKING-OUT HAIR, MAYBE WEARING BOOTS AND POSSIBLY CAPES MADE FROM FLAGS?

YOU MEAN THE HALFWAY HOUSE?

BUS STOP

A LADY TOLD *me* TO GET OFF AT A *certain* STOP WHERE *I'd* FIND THE HALFWAY HOUSE. I ASKED *her* IF *it* WAS LIKE *the* HOUSE OF THE RISING SUN. SHE SAID IT *was* IF THAT WAS *also* A PLACE FOR PEOPLE *who* WERE OUT OF THEIR *heads.* IT SOUNDED *right.*

When I FIRST SAW *the* HALFWAY HOUSE, *I* THOUGHT I FOUND THEM. THERE *were* PEOPLE ON *the* FRONT STEPS. ONE HAD *a* GUITAR. ONE *had* A HAT *made* OF TIN FOIL. ONE GAVE ME THE PEACE SIGN *and beckoned me* OVER. THE *sun* WAS GOING DOWN. *I* WAS A LONG WAY FROM *home.*

THOSE PEOPLE ARE LIVING IN ANOTHER WORLD.

YEAH, THEY'RE GETTING GROOVY.

WHATEVER THEY'RE GETTING, JUST DON'T GIVE ME NONE.

HEY, LITTLE MAMA. GIMME A CIGARETTE AND I'LL WRITE A SONG ABOUT CHA.

YOU 'N' ME, DARLIN,' BEEN WAITIN' FOR YA.

I NOTICED A PEE SMELL. I NOTICED their FREAKED-out DOG EYES. ONE GUY made SOME WEIRD FINGER GESTURES and STARTED vomiting. I RAN. IT was NIGHT WHEN I GOT BACK TO MY street. THE CORNER WAS DEAD. THE kickball GAME was OVER. MY MOM WAS on THE FRONT PORCH SCREAMING.

I'M GOING TO KILL YOU! WHERE HAVE YOU BEEN?! N'AKO, I'M GOING TO KILL YOU!

Was IT SUMMER when THE GOLD-RUSH STARTED? PEOPLE CROSSING a CONTINENT with EXPANDING DREAMS. SAN FRANCISCO, MOM. That's WHERE I WAS. AND I LOST EVERYTHING. I'M READY to start 7TH GRADE.

GLADYS. HEY, GLADYS.

HEY.

Analyze

(1) What does San Francisco represent for the protagonist of this comic, the girl nicknamed N'ako? What type of community and values does she imagine she will find there?

(2) Gladys calls her best friend a "traitor." In what way is N'ako a traitor? And to whom or what? Is the term "traitor" meant to be ironic?

(3) The text at the top of each panel is called a "caption." A caption usually presents information that would be difficult to include in either action or dialogue. What is the relationship between the text in the captions and the text within the dialogue bubbles? Is the voice of the captions an older voice than the voice of N'ako inside the comic? How would the comic change without captions?

(4) Barry's drawings in this story are raw and somewhat unrealistic. In an interview, she once described her style as "scribbly." What effects does this visual style have on the meaning or "feel" of the story?

Explore

(1) Of all the panels in this story, which seems to be the most crucial? What alerts you to its importance—text, image, or some other graphic or narrative element?

(2) Create one additional panel that goes either before the start of this piece or after it. Include both the artwork and the text (don't forget the caption at the top of each panel as well as the dialogue bubbles). Consider what your panel might add to the story to enhance and deepen its presentation.

(3) The song N'ako recalls with the "sad, beautiful melody" is most likely Scott McKenzie's "If You're Going to San Francisco." Find this song on YouTube or another free online music site—it's readily available. After listening to it, reread the comic. In what way do the song and its lyrics affect your understanding of the story?

(4) Broken dreams and painful disappointments are a part of childhood. In a narrative essay, tell the story of a childhood disappointment that was important to you. Use specific language and concrete details to clearly capture your experience—as clearly as Lynda Barry captured the experience of N'ako in the graphic comic "San Francisco." Explore the importance of this disappointment. How did you grow from it? What did you learn about yourself or the complexities of the larger world?

GABRIELLE BELL

"When I Was Eleven"

Gabrielle Bell was born in England, but at the age of two, she moved to Northern California with her mother. She attended Humboldt State University and City College of San Francisco, where she studied art. In 1998 she began to self-publish her comics in yearly collections. Her art fluctuates between surrealism and realist line drawings. More so than most contemporary comic artists, her understanding of narrative is strongly related to the traditions of the American short story. As such, our textbook includes more than one entry by Gabrielle Bell. Presently she lives in Brooklyn, New York.

WHEN I WAS ELEVEN

We lived twenty miles outside of a small town with no electricity, no phone, and no visitors my age. Summers were long and dreary.

MOM, I'M BORED!

READ A BOOK.

I'VE READ THEM ALL, TWICE!

WELL...

ENJOY NATURE.

I'M TIRED OF NATURE!

That changed when I went to summer camp at a nearby commune.

There was no difficulty, no boredom, just fun thing after fun thing all day.

I SHOULD REMEMBER THIS FEELING I HAVE NOW. I'LL FREEZE THIS MOMENT IN MY MIND AND SAVE IT FOR LATER

And at school.

EW, IT'S GABRIE-SMELL!

WHAT IS HER PROBLEM?

So one morning I filled my bag with food and books and clothes...

GOING TO THE HOG FARM, GABRIELLE?

YEAH.

MY DAD'S DOING SOME WORK OVER THERE.

Young Adulthood

Analyze

(1) Based on the information in the comic, why is Gabrielle unhappy at home? Does her unhappiness seem excessive?

(2) Gabrielle expresses a desire to be around kids her own age, a desire that is fulfilled at camp. Yet she does not like being around kids her own age at school. In your opinion, does camp primarily fulfill Gabrielle's need to be around others her own age? Or does it fulfill some other, unspecified need?

(3) The camp experience was a good one for Gabrielle, but afterward, she felt her life at home was more difficult to endure. In your opinion, would it have been better for Gabrielle to have never experienced camp or was it better that she experienced camp even if it deepened her discontent with her home life?

(4) Discuss Gabrielle's feeling toward her father in the final panel. Has her father earned Gabrielle's hostility? Or is Gabrielle using anger to some other end— to create an identity outside her family, to establish personal space for herself, to test her parents' love, and so on?

Explore

(1) "When I Was Eleven" is a comic memoir, meaning that the comic is a collection of the author's memories expressed in graphic form. As a reader, how do your expectations for a "true" story differ from one that is largely made up? What qualities do you look for in a story of memoir as opposed to one of fiction?

(2) Gabrielle objects to her parents' alternate lifestyle—living without electricity and phone in a rural setting. In four or five informal paragraphs, discuss one aspect of your family's lifestyle that you greatly appreciated and one that you, as a young adult, desperately wanted to change.

(3) At the age of eleven, Gabrielle finds personal growth and satisfaction at camp, where, for many days, she lives away from her family. Develop a list of five to seven qualities that you believe most young adults learn apart from their families. In your opinion, how do experiences outside a family help a young adult grow in ways that are difficult to reproduce inside the home?

(4) Gabrielle wants to freeze her experience at camp "and save it for later." Write an essay about a memory of emotional importance for you, one that you turn to when life is difficult or disappointing. What specifically does this memory offer you—strength, a sense of community or understanding, a feeling of warmth, a larger or more authoritative sense of yourself? And how does this past moment still play a role in your life?

DERF

"The Bank"

Derf is the pen name for the comic artist John Backderf. Born in 1959, Backderf grew up in Richfield, Ohio, and later attended the Art Institute of Pittsburgh and Ohio State University. As an artist, his images have appeared on T-shirts and CD covers, and in periodicals ranging from the *Wall Street Journal* to *Guitar Player*. He is best known for his weekly strip *The City*, which appeared in over 100 alt-weekly newspapers from 1990 to 2014. In addition to *The City* he has published graphic novels, including *My Friend Dahmer*, which recounts the author's childhood experience with Jeffrey Dahmer, a boy who would later become a serial killer and cannibal. Backderf presently lives in Cleveland, Ohio.

HEY OTTO! I JUST GOT OFF THE PHONE WITH THE MANAGER OF **THE CLASH!**

JINGLE TINKLE JINGLE

P.O.C. PREMIUM

P.O.C. PREMIUM

I CAN'T BELIEVE THE CLASH ARE PLAYING HERE!

THEY DRAW 100,000 FANS TO A GIG IN HYDE PARK IN LONDON...

JINGLE JINGLE

P.O.C. PREMIUM

C. PREMIUM

WHAM!!!

BUT OUT HERE IN MIDDLE AMERICA, THEY HAVE TO PLAY A MODEST CLUB LIKE THE BANK.

MEANWHILE... **JOURNEY** FILLS A 20,000-SEAT ARENA THE SAME WEEKEND!

LOOK ON THE BRIGHT SIDE! THANKS TO THE **APPALLING** TASTE OF THE AMERICAN PUBLIC, **WE** HAVE THE CLASH FOR TWO NIGHTS.

ANYWAYS...AS I WAS TRYING TO TELL YOU, THEIR MANAGER WANTS **YOU** TO CHAUFFEUR THE BOYS AROUND AKRON! THEY'RE INTO 'EXPERIENCING' AMERICA THIS TOUR. SO BE CREATIVE. THEY GET IN THE DAY BEFORE THE FIRST SHOW.

EXCELLENT! I LOVE TO CHAUFFEUR.

ALL TH' BANDS DEMAND YOUR SERVICES. YER A LEGEND!

YES, BUT THAT WAS INEVITABLE.

OH...ONE MORE THING... THERE'S A **DEAD RAT** IN THE MENS' ROOM URINAL. FRAID I GOTTA ASK YOU TO TAKE CARE OF IT.

GIGGLE. **ONE** MINUTE THE CONSORT OF ROCK STARS, THE **NEXT**...

SORRY ABOUT THAT, BABY.

WELL, THAT'S **PROBABLY** A METAPHOR FOR SOMETHING... BUT I DON'T REALLY CARE TO DECIPHER IT.

P.O.C.

P.O.C.

SIGH.

ROCK AND ROLL.

Young Adulthood

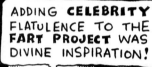

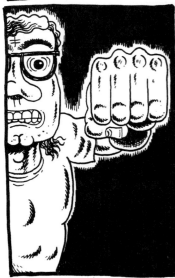

Young Adulthood

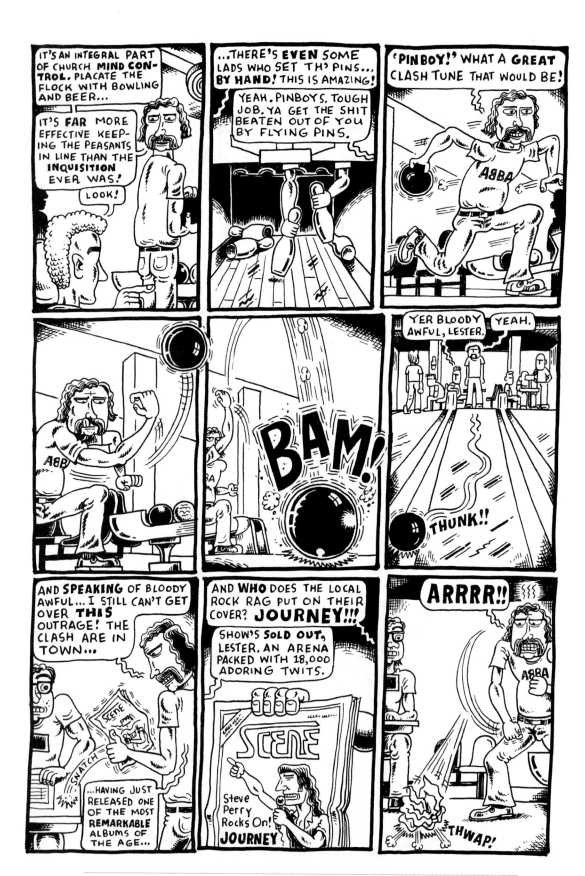

THESE INTENTIONAL CRIPPLES WHO WOULD GIDDILY GO TO A JOURNEY CONCERT... WE NEED TO **KICK** THEM **AWAKE!**

THESE ARE **MUTANT TIMES!** WE NEED PEOPLE MAKING PASSIONATE MUSIC OUT OF **NOISE** AND **SONIC SCRAPS!**

INSTEAD WE GET STEVE PERRY CROONING **BANAL FLAPDOODLE** TO THRONGS OF MESMERIZED SHEEP!

YEAH!!! PREACH **TH' WORD,** BRUTHA LESTER!

SIGH.

YA KNOW... I'VE BEEN WRITING ABOUT THIS FOR 15 YEARS... URGING MALLEABLE YOUTHS TO IMMERSE THEMSELVES IN **LOU REED... IGGY POP... PUBLIC IMAGE, LTD... THE CLASH...**

NO ONE IS LISTENING.

OUR RECORD STORES ARE FESTOONED WITH MAMMOTH DISPLAYS HAWKING THE LATEST VOMIT SPEWED UP BY **BOSTON** AND **STYX.**

OUR AIRWAVES ARE CLOGGED WITH THE SYPHILITIC SOUNDS OF THE **EAGLES** AND **POCO!!**

WE **CAN'T** MAKE A BETTER RECORD... AND RADIO HERE IN THE STATES **STILL** WON'T PLAY OUR SONGS. IN BRITAIN, THE KIDS **DEMAND** OUR MUSIC...

BUT **HERE.**

BUT **HERE**... THAT SAME GENERATION OF KIDS ARE RALLYING IN HUGE NUMBERS TO ELECT A OVER-POMPADOURED MONKEY FUCKER IN **RONALD REAGAN!**

AAAAR!! DON'T SAY HIS NAME!

JOURNEY... REAGAN... IT'S **ALL** PART OF THE SAME VAST CONSPIRACY TO ENCOURAGE AMERICANS TO VOLUNTARILY **SELF-LOBOTOMIZE** FOR THE NEW DECADE!

WE **CAN'T** DO ANYTHING TO STOP RONNIE...

BUT IF YOU WANNA **DERAIL** THE ROCK-N-ROLL CORPORATE JUGGERNAUT... YOU **DON'T** DO IT BY APPEALLING TO AMERICANS INTELLECTUALLY, **THAT'S** FOR SURE!

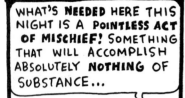
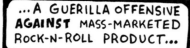

204

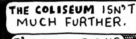

Analyze

(1) John "Derf" Backderf claims that his artistic style was largely influenced by the punk movement of the 1970s, which relied on expressionism and subjectivity to convey an alternate sense of reality through art. How is the emotional presentation of Backderf's line drawings different from those of the other texts in this chapter?

(2) "The Bank" mixes invented fictional characters (such as Otto) with historic celebrities (such as the rock critic Lester Bangs and Joe Strummer of the Clash). In the world of traditional novels, this mixture is termed "historical fiction." As this story is largely invented, what qualities can this comic of historical fiction deliver to an audience beyond that of straight history? That is, why did the author choose to explore the early 1980s through a mix of history and fiction rather than simply conveying the actual events of Joe Strummer's or Lester Bang's lives in graphic form?

(3) Otto suggests that mischief can be a form of art. What does he mean by that? How does mischief communicate a message or place viewers in a state of contemplation similar to that of painting or sculpture?

(4) In the world of "The Bank," wealth and class status don't much matter to Otto, Lester, and Joe. What values matter to these characters? What makes them feel successful?

Explore

(1) Otto, Joe, and Lester Bangs bemoan that Americans are forced to listen to bland, corporate rock while political and artistic musicians are marginalized because they don't have the connections or money to effectively promote their music. Develop a list of three contemporary musicians or bands that you would define as "corporate." Also develop a list of three musicians or bands whose music you would describe as more meaningful. What makes their music more meaningful—originality in melody, honesty in lyrics, inventive use of harmonies or instrumentation, political orientation of its message, and so on?

(2) The vision of American life in Backderf's comic differs vastly from Gabrielle Bell's. Backderf details the seediness of city life by including unappealing visual elements (rats, farts, urinals, etc.), and his characters are often troubled by facial sweat, acne, and obesity. Which do you believe presents a more honest and authentic vision of American life, Backderf's or Bell's?

(3) In the comic, Otto attempts to protest against the corporatization of music through an act of vandalism, an act without language. Write an essay about an experience in which you (perhaps with a group of friends) attempted to communicate a message in a medium that did not use language. This might include a flash mob, a series of paintings, a webpage, an Internet meme, an instrumental song, a photograph, and so on. In your essay also explore how the power of nonverbal communication differs from that of verbal communication, particularly as it relates to your actions.

KEVIN MUTCH

"Blue Note" (excerpt from *Fantastic Life*)

Kevin Mutch earned an MFA in painting at the University of Victoria in 1990 and at one time worked as the art director for the band Crash Test Dummies. Originally from Winnipeg, Canada, Mutch now lives in New York City, where he works as a digital artist. In this excerpt from his full-length graphic novel *Fantastic Life*, a young slacker experiences a powerful combination of drinking, drugs, music, and philosophy.

Young Adulthood

Analyze

(1) How does the introduction of mind-altering drugs affect the narrative? How would the story be different if Adam didn't eat the hash brownie or drink alcohol?

(2) In your own words, what type of commentary does Mutch seem to be making about young slackers? About music? About philosophy?

(3) How would you describe the drawing style Mutch uses? Why do you think he chose that option versus a more realistic or classical approach?

(4) Are his social interactions portrayed positively or negatively? What's the evidence you find in the story to support your ideas?

Explore

(1) Write a short response that explores the differences between Adam's internal thoughts and the actual dialogue he has with women. Which is more interesting? Which is more honest? Which is more compelling to you, the reader? If we had access to just the internal or external, how would the story change?

(2) What examples from popular culture speak to the type of slacker Adam appears to be? How do those examples differ from Adam?

(3) Research whether Adam is correct in his explanation about Niels Bohr's ideas of the universe. Is Adam right? Does the meaning of the story change if he is or isn't?

(4) In no more than two pages, illustrate what you think happens next in the story through a series of graphic novel panels. Include internal and external dialogue as needed. (Significant drawing skill is not required to effectively extend this storyline.) After you've created your addition to the story, consider sharing it with a friend and discussing the differences. You might also want to find a copy of Mutch's *Fantastic Life* to compare yours to.

JONATHAN BENNETT

"Dance With The Ventures"

Not to be confused with the actor Jonathan Bennett (who starred in *Mean Girls* and numerous other movie and TV shows) or the Australian writer Jonathan Bennett, the author of "Dance With The Ventures" studied printmaking at the Hartford Art School. A self-professed "comics geek," he lives in Brooklyn and designs book covers for St. Martin's Press in New York City. His story "Dance With The Ventures" chronicles the quiet life of a young man who is comfortable with "dumpster diving." This city-dweller runs into an older man whom he sees as a possible future self, and in so doing, he glimpses a future that might inform how he chooses to live his life today.

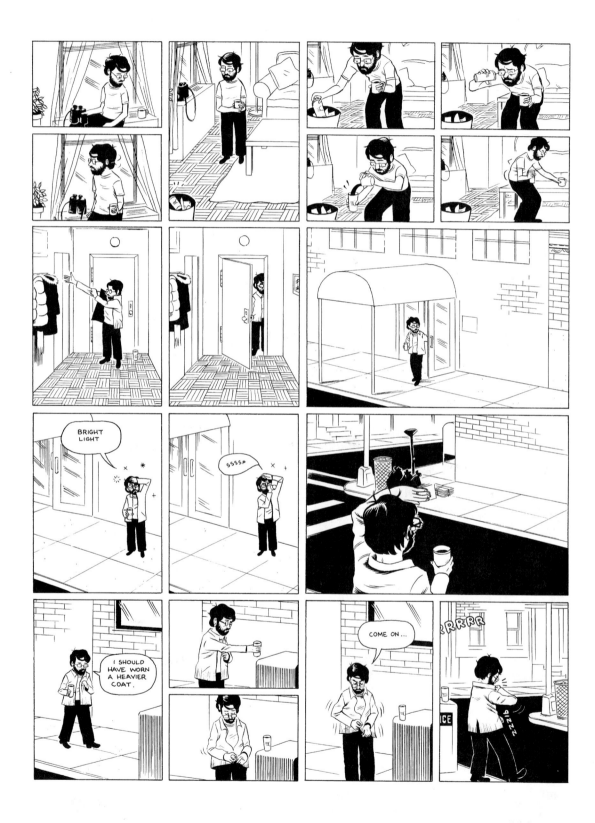

Young Adulthood

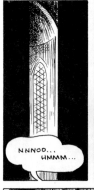

Young Adulthood

Young Adulthood

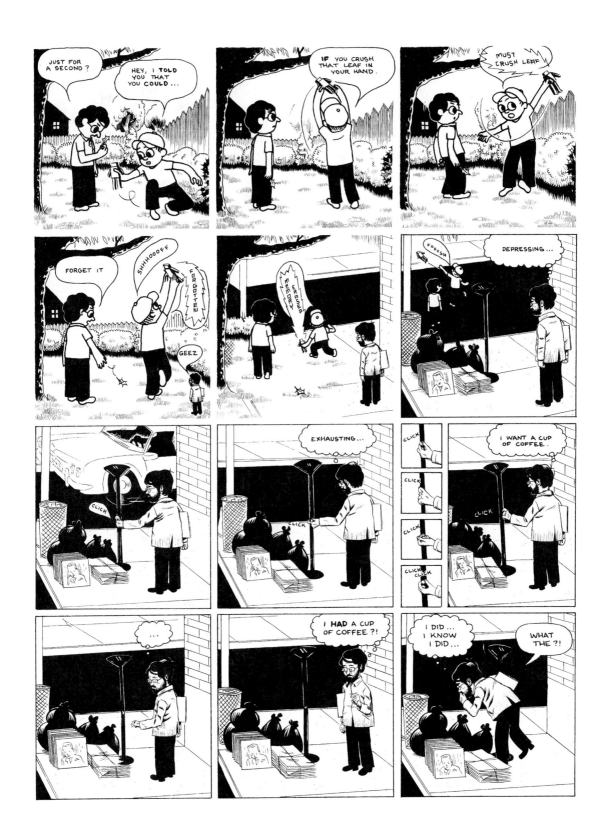

Young Adulthood

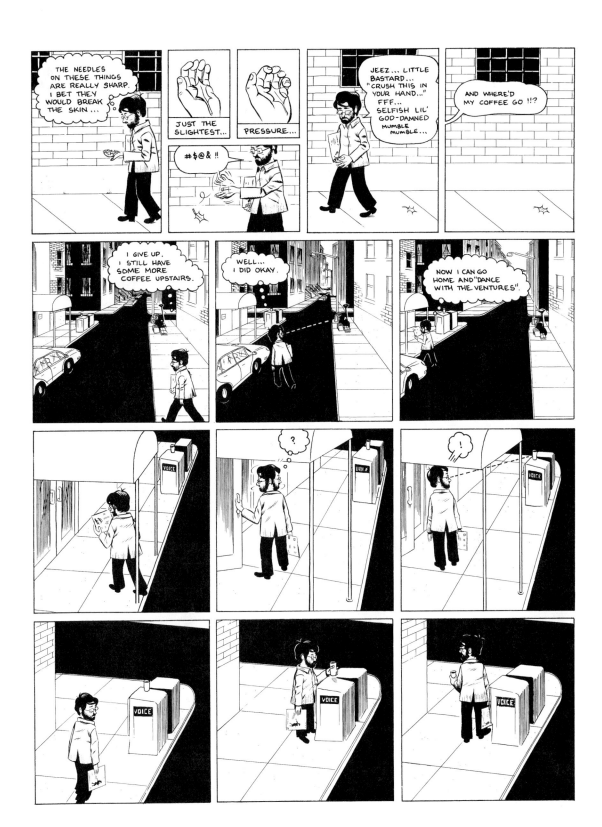

Analyze

(1) This story embraces the idea of quiet more so than many other stories. Why do so many panels contain no words? How does this affect the way you read the story? What does all that silence mean in terms of the protagonist's life? His past? His future?

(2) What is the purpose of the flashback in the middle of the story? What do you believe the author wanted readers to take away from that glimpse at the protagonist's early childhood?

(3) There is an economy and sparseness to both the language and the art in this story. How does that play into the tone and atmosphere?

(4) If a story is about conflict, where do you see conflict (or conflicts) here? What's at stake? Who wins? Who loses?

Explore

(1) The Ventures were an actual music group in the 1960s. Take a moment to find out more about them and their surprising popularity and longevity. Why does the author use the Ventures versus another 1960s group such as Simon & Garfunkel or Pink Floyd? What does it mean that it's actually a folk singer's record in the sleeve of the Ventures album? Why call the piece "Dance with the Ventures" then?

(2) Write a short essay that examines the prominent role of garbage in this story. In what way does it link up with theme and meaning? Be sure to address the idea of disposability and reclamation.

(3) Churches can serve as places of refuge, safety, and quiet personal introspection. Just as it happens in the story, one might also find a sympathetic kind person there who is willing to listen or help. Make a list of reasons the protagonist might have gone to the church versus another public building. In what way might it be important that his attention falls on church music considering the musical elements already included in this story?

(4) While Bennett always loved drawing, it wasn't until he encountered Seth's *It's a Good Life*, which he devoured in one sitting during a long train ride, that he realized he, too, would be able to create his own graphic tales. Find examples of the comic artist Seth's work online and then write a short essay that examines the influence Seth's work has had on Bennett's.

Trauma

One observation about trauma remains profoundly true: nothing properly prepares you for it. Whether you've suffered a car crash, experienced the loss of a loved one, or witnessed a shooting, the tragedy often comes without warning. Worse, life goes on while you are forced to deal with the aftermath.

In the most general sense of the word, "trauma" can refer to both the damage inflicted and the person's emotional response to it. Quite often psychological damage is more debilitating than a puncture wound or a broken bone. Just observe any soldier who's suffered from posttraumatic stress disorder or an abused child who has withdrawn from the world in a final act of self-preservation. The literature of trauma, then, explores human responses to devastating injury and debilitating experience.

Examples of trauma, in its literary sense, would include the following:

- The Holocaust
- The refugee experience
- War and its aftermath
- 9/11 and other terrorist attacks
- Sexual abuse or violence
- Domestic violence
- Exposure to acts of violence
- Death of a loved one
- School shootings
- Natural disasters
- Other devastating events

It's no surprise, then, that artists and writers spend a lot of time examining damage, the terrible interruption of an otherwise normal life. They likely subscribe to the idea of trauma that Sarah Hackley writes about in the essay collection *Women Will Save the World*: "Past traumas are like old scars that never quite healed properly—they occasionally must be cut open, re-examined, and sutured anew."

The following selections do exactly that: they reveal the massive psychic shocks trauma victims experience and observe how our culture regards trauma and traumatized people. All too often, those who experience trauma are implicitly or even explicitly blamed for their own fates—as if the same couldn't happen to the rest of us!

Consider Miriam Engelberg's memoir in comics, *Cancer Made Me a Shallower Person*. In a painfully honest narrative, she details the deterioration of her life after being diagnosed with breast cancer at age forty-three. Compare that to the excerpt from *The Alcoholic* by Jonathan Ames and Dean Haspiel, in which the authors juxtapose personal damage against the public events of 9/11. Both stories examine tragedy in a deeply personal manner, though each version has a far different commentary on the realities of trauma.

Set against the turbulent background of the war-torn Balkans, Gipi's *Notes for a War Story* shows how three young drifters move from being victims of trauma to the cause of it for others. Joe Sacco's *Journalism* also reveals a wartime situation, only this one follows U.S. soldiers through the misery and horrors of the war in Iraq. And in *Harlem Hellfighters*—a fictionalized account of the 369th Infantry Regiment, the first African-American regiment in World War I—Max Brooks imagines the enlistment lines in Harlem to the deadly futures that await these men.

As you encounter these selections, pay particular attention to the presentation of trauma. Ask yourself, what comments, arguments, and statements is the author putting forth? And what thematic issues do trauma stories handle more effectively than other stories do? Finally, think about the philosophical, political, and historical context in each narrative. How do these elements add to the impact of the stories?

BROOKS AND WHITE

The Harlem Hellfighters

The son of Mel Brooks and actress Anne Bancroft, Max Brooks spent three years writing for *Saturday Night Live* in the early 2000s. However, he's best known for his Zombie Survival Guide books and the book and film versions of *World War Z: An Oral History of the Zombie War*. Brooks has worked as an actor on episodes of *7th Heaven*, *Roseanne*, and *Pacific Blue*, and has done voice-over work for *Batman Beyond*, *Justice League*, and *All Dogs Go to Heaven: The Series*.

Illustrator Caanan White has worked with some of the top graphic novel publishers—Dabel Brothers, Marvel Comics, and Avatar Press. His blend of realism and detail earned him the illustration job for the *Uber* series, an alternative history of World War II in which Hitler gains the upper hand. White followed that up with his work on *The Harlem Hellfighters*, a fictionalized account of the 369th Regiment in World War I, an African-American group of soldiers who saw more combat time than any other unit.

Trauma

       Trauma

FAMINE.

DISEASE...

EVEN ONE CASE OF MASS MURDER THAT'D ONE DAY BE CALLED "GENOCIDE."*

*THE EXTERMINATION OF ARMENIAN CIVILIANS BY THE OTTOMAN EMPIRE.

AND THOSE WERE JUST CIVILIANS. IF YOU LUMP THEM ALL IN WITH THE ACTUAL "BATTLEFIELD CASUALTIES,"

...ALL THE POOR SLOBS WHO FOLLOWED THEIR FLAGS INTO BATTLE...

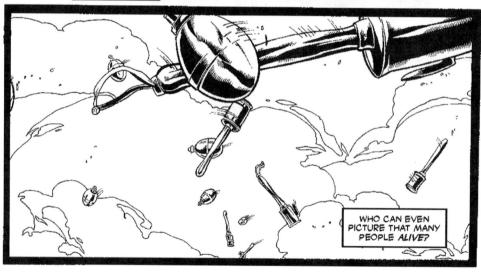

Trauma

Trauma

HE KNEW WE'D HAVE TO JUMP INTO THE FIRE SOMEDAY. THE QUESTION WAS, HOW TO SELL IT TO THE REST OF US?

WHY WOULD AMERICANS WANNA GET ALL MUDDY AND BLOODY "OVER THERE"?

NOT FOR LAND, NOT FOR TREASURE, WE HAD ALL WE NEEDED "OVER HERE."

"THE SCHOOLMASTER" KNEW THAT BETTER THAN ANYONE. HE FIGURED AMERICANS WOULD ONLY FIGHT FOR SOMETHING BIGGER THAN OURSELVES, A HIGHER CALLING, A GREAT CRUSADE.

AND THAT'S WHEN I ANSWERED THE CALL.

THAT'S WHEN I FIRST MET THE 15TH NEW YORK NATIONAL GUARD REGIMENT, THE "BLACK RATTLERS"...

"Colored man is no slacker."

...ON THE SECOND FLOOR OF A DANCE STUDIO IN HARLEM, NEW YORK.

Trauma

AND ME...

I GREW UP JUST TWO BLOCKS FROM HERE...

...AND NOW IT FELT LIKE ANOTHER PLANET.

JOININ' SOMETHING BIGGER THAN YOURSELF CAN MAKE YOU FEEL MIGHTY SMALL

DESMOND SCATLIFFE, FROM THE DANISH WEST INDIES.

AND SO THE DANISH WEST INDIES BECAME THE U.S. VIRGIN ISLANDS, BUT THE LOCALS WOULDN'T BE COUNTED AS CITIZENS FOR ANOTHER TEN YEARS.

THEY'D JUST BECOME A U.S. TERRITORY, MAINLY 'CAUSE UNCLE SAM DIDN'T WANT THEM, DENMARK WAS 'SPOSED TO BE NEUTRAL IN THIS WAR, BUT THEN AGAIN, SO WERE WE.

I'M NOT SURE IF DES EVER KNEW THAT...

...OR WOULDA CARED.

PARTNER, AIN' YOU KNOW YOUR HISTORY?

Trauma

Trauma

Analyze

(1) Caanan White has the ability to produce ultra-realistic illustrations that are as arresting as photography. For this book, though, while his illustrations are realistic, they are not photorealistic. Why did he make that choice? Is there something counterintuitive going on whereby the more realistic the images on the page, the less meaning a reader can extract from it? Scott McCloud discusses this phenomenon at length in his book *Understanding Comics*. He offers a number of reasons for this, but one explanation is that "the more cartoony a face is, for instance, the more people it could be said to describe"; it creates universality. Do you believe that White was striving for universality when creating these panels? Or do you see some other motivation beneath White's style?

(2) What power structures are evident in the story? Do they change along the way? How do the characters react to those structures?

(3) It's often challenging for writers to accurately depict events of racial significance for characters outside of their own cultural experience. Early in this story, we find references to black characters "fresh off the banana boat" and a Pullman porter who says, "And one ah them medal a' honors!" Are these expressions problematic? Or are they an attempt to include period-specific dialogue? Does this story effectively explore issues of race in a way that avoids racism? Why or why not?

Explore

(1) What do you and your peers already know about World War I? If you were writing a graphic narrative about this subject, how would you handle any possible gaps in reader knowledge? How did Brooks and White handle it?

(2) How important is it that a fictional story based on historical happenings be well researched? Doesn't the idea of it being fiction supersede any obligation to historical reality? For Brooks's own opinion on this, watch the April 2014 video of him on BOOKTV discussing *The Harlem Hellfighters*. The fifty-four-minute video is free and readily found online. (There's also an uncorrected transcript of the Closed Captioning Record available as well.)

(3) This story, in part, explores labels, bullying, and injustice. These are experiences with which most students have some personal familiarity. What does this story add to what you already know about these issues?

(4) In an April 2014 *USA Today* interview, Brooks was asked how writing *World War Z* helped him dramatize real history. He replied, "I actually wrote the first draft of *The Harlem Hellfighters* (in screenplay format) years before *World War Z*. In fact, I wrote it even before *The Zombie Survival Guide*. *Harlem Hellfighters* has been with me for a very long time. Back in the '90s, I pitched the idea all over Hollywood. No one wanted it. I would have given up on it if LeVar Burton hadn't read it and told me to keep going." Have you ever had a project that you were committed to but the rest of the world wasn't? How did it turn out? Would it have been worth doing even if no one else seemed to care?

"Complacency Kills," from *Journalism*

Joe Sacco, a Maltese-American cartoonist and journalist, is one of the premiere comic journalists who covers conflict zones around the world. After earning a BA in journalism from the University of Oregon, he became disillusioned with the industry (he once called his experiences during that time as a series of "half-assed" reporting jobs) and returned to Malta, where he took up his childhood love of cartooning. He worked for a local guidebook publisher and published his own Maltese romance comic. Sacco then returned to the United States and worked for an alternative magazine out of Portland, Oregon, before becoming a staff writer for the *Comics Journal*. His interest in travel, however, took him back to Europe, and his experiences there led to his book *Palestine*.

Other books by Sacco include *Footnotes in Gaza*, *The Fixer*, and *Journalism*, from which the excerpt in this book is taken. With journalist Chris Hedges, he illustrated *Days of Destruction, Days of Revolt*, a book on U.S. poverty.

COMPLACENCY KILLS
by Joe Sacco ©2005
"When I'm on the road," says Sgt. Dance, commander of Mobile Assault Platoon (MAP) 4, explaining his policy toward Iraqi drivers here, "you're not on the road."
And so as we race to check on a report of some vehicles linking up in the middle of nowhere, the oncoming traffic had better get out of the way!
Lance Cpl. Janigo, binoculars pressed to his face, yells—
SINGLE!
—and Lance Cpl. Battles, the driver, flashes his lights until the startled Iraqi swerves off the road.
A single Iraqi in a car fits their profile of a suicide bomber, and our Humvee barely whizzes by that potential threat when two more cars come flying our way from under a bridge.
There's no time for Lance Cpl. Janigo to adjust his binoculars or for Lance Cpl. Battles to flash his lights!
Sgt. Dance screams—
GET 'EM OFF THE ROAD!
GET 'EM OFF THE ROAD!
—and Lance Cpl. Clark fires a burst across the front of the first car!
Both vehicles veer to a stop, and I catch a glimpse of a man with a moustache as we punch by.
J. SACCO 1-05

A few minutes later we reach the suspicious group of cars, which turns out to be a funeral procession.

"The bad guys don't usually congregate in vehicles on the side of the road," says Sgt. Dance, who was skeptical all along. "It's painfully obvious."

And to the bereaved he adds—

OUR SYMPATHIES ARE WITH YOU.

The primary mission of Sgt. Dance and the MAPs of the Weapons Company of the 1st Battalion, 23rd Marine Regiment is to keep the roads between Haditha and Hit open to U.S. convoys.

Their adversaries are insurgents whose chief weapons are roadside and vehicle-borne bombs and land mines. Twisted bits of car metal, charred patches of ground, and craters attest to the violence they've dished out to the Americans.

The Marines of the 1/23, who are nearly all Texan reservists, run most of their road patrols in this stretch of western Iraq from the functioning ten-story high Haditha Dam on the Euphrates River.

The stairwells reek of sulfur, but the Marines are otherwise smothered in home comforts: They enjoy a well-equipped weight room,

football on the chow hall's big-screen TV, and 24-hour internet connections to their wives and mothers.

I'm bunking on the fifth deck in a room full of officers where Lt. Crabtree, the battalion adjutant, projects a movie on the wall every night and dispenses snacks from an endless supply of pooled care packages.

The room's coffee aficionado is the commander of the engineering platoon, Capt. Kuniholm, and once I ask what motivated a married, liberal, business-owning Ph.D. student like himself to join the reserves knowing full well he would be sent to Iraq. A sense of duty, he answers.

Also—

YOU SHOULDN'T DISCOUNT THE SPIRIT OF WHITE, UPPER-MIDDLE CLASS ADVENTURISM.

Almost discordantly in this cocooned world of X-Boxes and Maxim magazines, a sign on the second deck reminds the Marines of the MAPs heading down to their Humvees that—

COMPLACENCY KILLS

J. SACCO 1.08

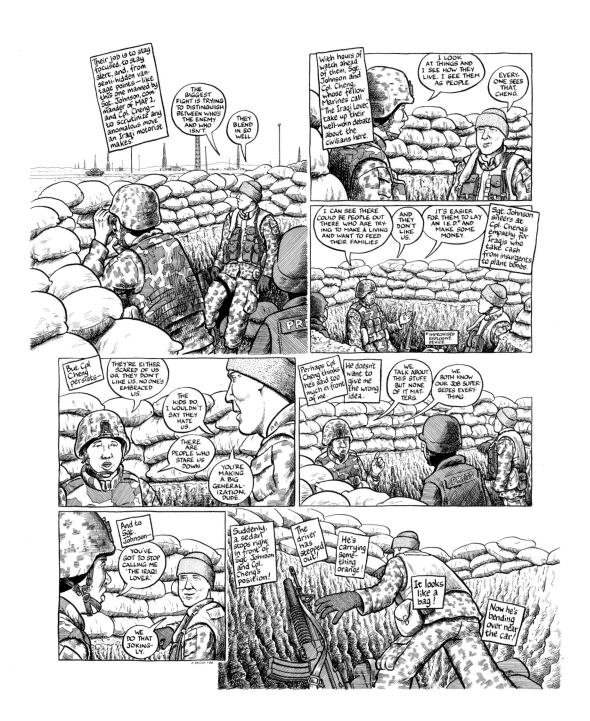

Trauma

Trauma

Analyze

(1) There are lots of captions on each page, but there isn't much dialogue. Does this suggest that this is a quiet environment? Does it put extra emphasis on dialogue when it's encountered? How important are the captions to this story?

(2) While this particular story is titled "Complacency Kills," it's from the book *Journalism*. What does the word "journalism" mean to you? And how might a journalistic approach to this topic differ from other accounts of this story? What's journalistic in the way Sacco handles things?

(3) You can always tell which character's Sacco—he's the one with the blank glasses. Find him in that dark panel in the middle of the second page. Why do his glasses look the way they do? Reviewers have noted that in many of Sacco's works, his own character is always a bit more cartoony than others. Why might that be so?

(4) How does the ending provide closure for the story? And why does the ending echo an earlier caption, one originally placed at the bottom of the first page?

Explore

(1) "When I'm on the road, you're *not* on the road," says Sgt. Dance at the start of this piece. Yes, that's his own policy toward Iraq, but how much does it reflect U.S. policy toward Iraq? If you're unsure of the explicit or implicit policies regarding Iraq during this time, do a little research or ask someone older about their memories of this period. What do you think of these policies?

(2) If you had to write a three-page (minimum) graphic narrative, how would you go about it? What would be your exact process of planning, writing, and revising? How fast would it be? Learn Sacco's surprising process in a June 2011 interview with the *Believer* magazine, which is free and readily available online.

(3) One thing that a writer always considers is audience. What considerations do you make when you write for a specific audience? Who do you imagine is the intended audience for this comic?

(4) In a July/August 2005 interview with *Mother Jones*, Sacco articulates the advantages of comic journalism: "It's a visual world and people respond to visuals. With comics you can put interesting and solid information in a format that's pretty palatable. For me, one advantage of comic journalism is that I can depict the past, which is hard to do if you're a photographer or filmmaker. History can make you realize that the present is just one layer of a story. What seems to be the immediate and vital story now will one day be another layer in this geology of bummers." Take a few moments to research one or two other comic journalists and then answer these questions: Journalists traditionally rely on text and photographs—elements that often carry the cultural authority of "truth." In your opinion what can comics contribute to journalism; what explorations or insights might be more effectively presented by a comic journalist than a traditional (textual) journalist or a photojournalist?

GIPI

Notes for a War Story

Gian Alfonso Pacinotti—known as "Gipi—is an Italian author, cartoonist, and filmmaker. His illustration career began in the 1960s and his illustrations have appeared in such periodicals and newspapers as *Boxer, Cuore, Blue,* and *La Repubblica.* While Gipi has been incredibly popular in Europe, it wasn't until his graphic novels *Notes for a War Story* (2004) and *Garage Band* (2005) were translated into English that he became a household name in the United States. His science fiction film *The Last Man on Earth* premiered at the 68th Venice International Film Festival.

Trauma

FELIX CAME BACK AT THE BEGINNING OF SPRING.

HE SEEMED TO HAVE AGED FIFTEEN YEARS.

AND YOU COULD PROBABLY SAY THE SAME ABOUT US.

THAT NIGHT AT THE ODEON THEATER WAS A LONG TIME AGO.

A LOT HAD HAPPENED.

LITTLE KILLER HAD COACHED US IN EVERY TYPE OF CRIME.

AND WE HAD ALWAYS FOLLOWED HIM FAITHFULLY.

HEY, STEFANO, AT LAST WE MEET AGAIN.

HI.

IT WAS BECAUSE OF HIM THAT WE HAD SO MUCH MONEY, A NICE PLACE TO LIVE, AND SMART CLOTHES.

HOW ARE YOU, FELIX?

HOW AM I?

CHRISTIAN HADN'T YET MANAGED TO BUY HIS DREAM MOTORCYCLE.

BUT WE COULDN'T COMPLAIN.

LOOK WHAT THEY DID TO MY FACE.

IT LOOKS LIKE JUST A SCRATCH, BUT THOSE SONS OF BITCHES TOOK AN EYE OUT.

GET IT?

WHERE'S THE DALMATIAN?

DIDN'T HE COME?

THE DALMATIAN'S SUFFERING HAS COME TO AN END.

AND HOW ARE YOU GUYS?

RUMORS HAVE BEEN GOING AROUND. I WAS WORRIED.

RUMORS?

THAT YOU MADE QUITE A FEW ENEMIES.

A FEW.

UH UH

HAS LITTLE KILLER GROWN?

I DON'T KNOW.

YOU'RE TALLER, I'M TELLING YOU.

WERE YOU SICK? DID YA HAVE A FEVER?

NO.

BUT YOU'VE GONE BLOND.

GOOD JOB.

YOU'VE DONE WELL.

THE BEST PEOPLE I KNOW ARE ALL BLOND.

LET'S GO.

I'LL TAKE YOU TO THE SEAFOOD PLACE.

Trauma

THE RESTAURANT WAS RIGHT BY THE SEA.

THERE WAS A WARM BREEZE THAT PROBABLY COULD HAVE CURED ANYONE OF THEIR ILLS.

AND THE GUY SAYS: I CAN DO IMPRESSIONS!

STEFANO TOLD HIM EVERYTHING WE'D DONE.

EVERY- THING.

HE WAS LIKE A STUDENT RECITING A LIST OF ALL THE HOME- WORK HIS TEACHER HAD GIVEN HIM.

THE LOOK ON THE RUSSIAN'S FACE WHEN HIS GUN JAMMED.

NGH NGH

CLICK CLICK

HA HA HA

WELL DONE. NOW LISTEN UP.

ALL THESE THINGS YOU'VE DESCRIBED — DID YOU ENJOY THEM?

YES.

AND DO YOU ALSO LIKE BEING IN HIDING?

RISKING JAIL TIME?

DO YOU LIKE THAT TOO?

WHAT I MEAN IS, IF YOU COULD DO EVERYTHING YOU DO NOW, BUT IN A WORLD WITHOUT TROUBLES...

WOULD YOU STILL BE HAPPY?

SURE. A WORLD LIKE THAT'D BE GREAT, IF THERE WERE ONE.

THERE IS.

Gipi: *Notes for a War Story* 287

Trauma

Trauma

Trauma

Trauma

WE PAID FOR THE ROOM. WE CAUGHT THE BUS THAT WOULD TAKE US TO THE MEETING PLACE.

WE WERE TO BECOME MEMBERS OF A MILITIA IN A FACTION WHOSE NAME WE DIDN'T EVEN KNOW.

I COULDN'T SLEEP EVEN A SECOND. BUT NOT BECAUSE I WAS AFRAID OF LEAVING...

I WAS ANGRY ABOUT WHAT THEY'D SAID TO ME.

MY HEART FELT LIKE IT WAS POUNDING AGAINST MY THROAT.

FUCK IT ALL, THEN!

WHAT CAN I SAY? GO TO HELL!

NO, FELIX, YOU GO TO HELL!

WHAT THE HELL WERE WE DOING DEFENDING SAN VITO?!

AM I THE ONLY GUY AROUND HERE WITH ANY BALLS?

FELIX!

FELIX, IT'S US, WE'RE HERE NOW!

HUH? WHO'S THAT?!

OH, THREE KIDS I FOUND.

I GOTTA THINK TOO, UNDERSTAND? I GOTTA GO RECRUITING DOOR TO DOOR.

HEY, KILLER, YOU'RE THE GREATEST. YOU'RE GONNA SEE HOW WE HAVE FUN AROUND HERE.

Gipi: *Notes for a War Story*   295

GUYS, COME WITH ME.

IF IT WEREN'T FOR KIDS LIKE YOU, I DON'T KNOW HOW WE'D KEEP GOING IN THIS WAR.

SO, GOOD!

WE'RE FRIENDS OF FELIX.

AREN'T WE ALL.

COME IN, HERE'S YOUR STUFF.

AN AK-47, TWO MAGAZINES, A CANTEEN.

KILLER WANTED HAND GRENADES, BUT HE WAS TOLD THEY WERE ALL OUT.

WE EACH GOT A RIBBON TO TIE TO OUR RIGHT ARM AND WERE TOLD TO BE CAREFUL NOT TO GET THE ARMS MIXED UP.

WE'LL GO BACK TO THE SQUARE. I'LL SEE THAT YOU'RE PUT IN THE SAME SQUAD.

WHERE CAN I FIND FELIX?

HE'LL FIND YOU. HE'S GOT A TON OF THINGS TO DO RIGHT NOW.

AND THEN WHERE SHOULD WE GO?

Trauma

I RAN INTO THE FIELDS, RAN LIKE CRAZY THE ENTIRE NIGHT.

AND THEN?

I WENT BACK TO THE CITY AND FOUND MY PARENTS.

I HAD KEPT IT HIDDEN FROM THE OTHERS, BUT I DID KNOW WHERE TO FIND MY FAMILY.

I HAD PHONED THEM A COUPLE OF TIMES, TO TELL THEM I WAS ALIVE.

I HUNG UP WHEN THEY STARTED TO CRY.

STEFANO WAS RIGHT.

THERE WAS ANOTHER WAY FOR ME. I WASN'T LIKE THEM.

AND WHERE ARE YOUR FRIENDS NOW?

I DON'T KNOW.

THE LAST TIME I SAW THEM THEY WERE BEING TAKEN AWAY IN THE TRUCK.

Trauma

Trauma

Gipi: *Notes for a War Story*

Trauma

Notes for a War Story

Analyze

(1) The setting is an unnamed European country. Does it matter that it's not named? The story is about an unnamed conflict between unspecified groups. Do those omissions matter? Why do you think Gipi left these things unnamed? Does it matter that it's sometimes hard to tell the characters apart?

(2) The story isn't told in the form of notes—and there isn't that much war going on, though it seems to exist in the background. With these things in mind, what do you make of the title?

(3) From a pure design point of view, graphic communication is all about form, shape, lights, and darks. How would you describe the visual style of *Notes for a War Story*? Would you reference the bluish-gray tones? The sharp noses? The haircuts?

(4) Stories are about characters who change. Which characters seem to have changed? In what ways?

Explore

(1) Gipi is deeply concerned with truth. He's said, "I set a lot of rules for my work. I call them 'ethical rules.' Like the book *S.*, which I wrote in the past year, about my father and his life and death. In *S.*, I forced myself to write the text directly on the page, without any script—120 pages of improvisation without the possibility of corrections. It is a tribute to my father, so I don't want to be 'good' at telling his life. I was looking to create something, maybe badly made, but true." What do you feel is true about this story? Where in this story is the authority of truth most present?

(2) A morality play has come to mean an allegorical story in which characters are forced to make difficult moral choices. Here we have a lower-class sycophant, a poor criminal, and a wayward middle-class man all being challenged by circumstances. Through the actions of these characters, what does Gipi say about holding on to an old society versus embracing a new one? About remaining passive or active in a conflict?

(3) *Notes for a War Story* won the René Goscinny Prize for Best Script at the Angoulême International Comics Festival in 2005 and Best Book of the Year the following year. With these awards in mind, why do you believe critics felt this story should speak to a large audience?

(4) In an interview with Words Without Borders, Gipi confesses, "There is always a character who is dumber than the others. This is me. It's Julien (Giuliano) in *Notes for a War Story* and Julien again in *Garage Band*. I'm the dumbest character, the one who observes, who acts a little less than the others do." Is Gipi being overly harsh on himself? Do you find the Julien character to be easier to relate to than the others? Gipi goes on to add, "They're the narrators. It's my voice. That's the difference between Julien and the other characters. Julien watches the action; the others *do* things. Julien is never really living." What do you think Gipi means by that last statement?

AMES AND HASPIEL

The Alcoholic

A columnist for the *New York Press* for many years, Jonathan Ames is known for writing gritty, self-deprecating autobiographical stories. *The Alcoholic* was his first graphic novel, though he's written other novels before, such as *I Pass Like Night*, *Wake Up, Sir!*, and *The Extra Man*, which was made into a film starring Kevin Kline. Ames is also the author of *The Double Life Is Twice as Good*, a collection of essays and stories. *Bored to Death*, an HBO series that ran for two seasons, was also one of Ames's creations.

Dean Haspiel is an American comic book artist known for his collaborations with writers, including Harvey Pekar, Inverna Lockpez, Stan Lee, Jonathan Lethem, and, of course, Jonathan Ames. Haspiel received a 2010 Emmy for TV design work on Ames's *Bored to Death*. Graphic novel fans know Haspiel as the creator of Billy Dogma, the "last romantic anti-hero," who debuted in Haspiel's *Keyhole* and appeared in a number of stories and graphic novels since then.

Trauma

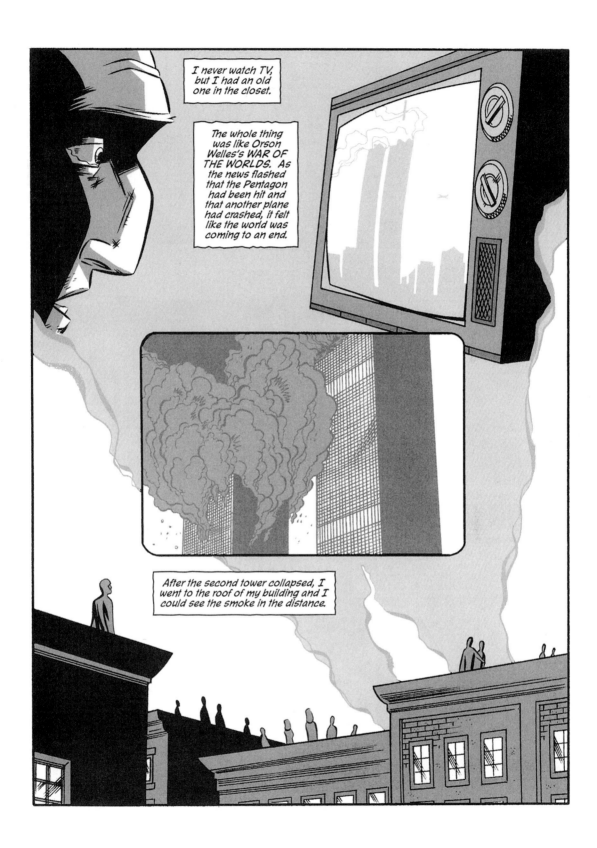

ARE YOU ALL RIGHT?

SOME PEOPLE IN THE NEIGHBORHOOD ARE GOING TO GIVE BLOOD, THEY'VE ASKED ME TO JOIN THEM.

BE CAREFUL! I LOVE YOU.

I LOVE YOU.

A bunch of writers in my neighborhood got together and we all went to the Hyatt where the Red Cross was set up to take blood.

But I still had coke in my system and maybe marijuana, too. I didn't know what to do--how could I, in front of these other people, refuse to give blood and confess to doing drugs?

And if I gave blood would it hurt someone to get coke-tainted TYPE A?

As it turned out, they couldn't take any more blood--so my own little self-centered crisis was averted.

In the lobby of the hotel, I spotted the famous author John Updike. I had seen him in Brooklyn before. It was somehow reassuring that a great writer was there.

John Updike

And Updike had just given blood. That's all anybody could think to do. Give blood. And, that, as we all know, turned out to be futile on 9/11. The blood wasn't needed. There were hardly any injuries, only fatalities.

I hadn't slept in 24 hours. Finally, in the afternoon, I passed out.

After sleeping for a few hours, I went back up to the roof.

JONATHAN, CAN YOU HELP ME? MARK WAS IN WINDOWS ON THE WORLD. I NEED TO GO TO THE CITY AND FIND THE MORGUE. WILL YOU COME WITH ME?

YES... OH, MY GOD...OF COURSE.

My neighbor's name was Ellen. Her baby was six months old. Her husband, Mark, a stockbroker, had filled in for a colleague at the last minute at some meeting in Windows on the World.

All of her family and his family were in Long Island--no one could get to her, the city was shut down, and so that's why she asked me to go with her into Manhattan. She got a neighbor to look after her baby.

Somehow the A train was still running.

Ellen felt like she had to do something, and the only thing she could think of was to find her husband's body, to see him one last time.

She was certain he was dead.

She had heard that a temporary morgue would be by the old warship, the Intrepid--I don't know where she heard this, but there was no morgue there. The city was empty--no cars, a few scattered people here and there.

GO TO BELLEVUE--THAT'S WHERE THEY'RE BRINGING THE BODIES.

We started walking east towards Bellevue. I remember we passed a restaurant where some people were outside eating. It was so strange, the world seemingly had come to an end, and yet some restaurants were still open.

It was like people dancing as the Titanic went down. What else was there to do?

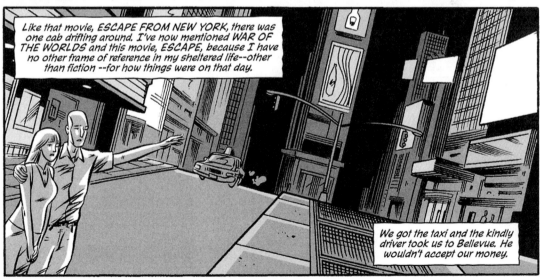

Like that movie, ESCAPE FROM NEW YORK, there was one cab drifting around. I've now mentioned WAR OF THE WORLDS and this movie, ESCAPE, because I have no other frame of reference in my sheltered life--other than fiction --for how things were on that day.

We got the taxi and the kindly driver took us to Bellevue. He wouldn't accept our money.

There were hundreds of weeping people in front of Bellevue. It was mass hysteria.

There were no bodies to be seen.

We found some random government worker who was writing down the names of missing people.

HIS NAME IS MARK DRISCOLL. HE WAS IN WINDOWS ON THE WORLD.

We waited about an hour and a half for a subway. Ellen was quiet almost the whole time.

Everything was so still. What was usually so ordinary--waiting for a subway now felt extraordinary. We were all so frightened.

HE WOULDN'T HAVE WANTED THIS. HE WOULDN'T HAVE WANTED THIS.

I KNOW.

I'M OKAY. I'M SORRY.

YOU DON'T HAVE TO BE SORRY.

I knew a little bit of what she was going through, having lost my parents the way I did, but I didn't say anything.

Trauma

Mary, our sweet neighbor, had dutifully been baby-sitting.

We had been neighbors for four years, but I had never been in Ellen's apartment before. I looked around--this is where Mark had lived. He would never return.

THANK YOU, JONATHAN.

I CAN STAY ON YOUR COUCH, IF YOU LIKE.

THAT'S ALL RIGHT. I'LL BE OKAY. MARY IS GOING TO STAY WITH ME.

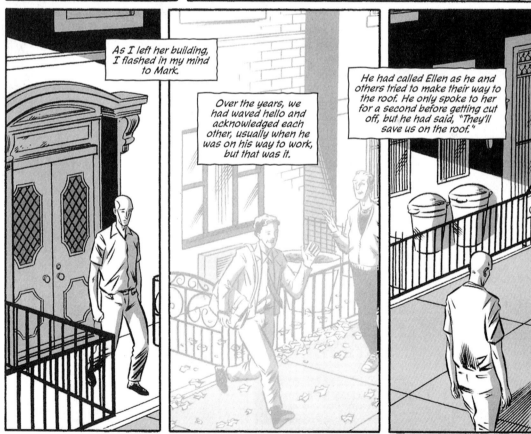

As I left her building, I flashed in my mind to Mark.

Over the years, we had waved hello and acknowledged each other, usually when he was on his way to work, but that was it.

He had called Ellen as he and others tried to make their way to the roof. He only spoke to her for a second before getting cut off, but he had said, "They'll save us on the roof."

I haven't really talked about politics in this tale, because I've always been somewhat apolitical, in much the same way that I'm agnostic.

But here's how I would summarize my general world-view: resigned, defeated, and heartbroken.

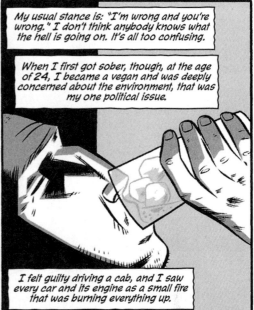

My usual stance is: "I'm wrong and you're wrong." I don't think anybody knows what the hell is going on. It's all too confusing.

When I first got sober, though, at the age of 24, I became a vegan and was deeply concerned about the environment, that was my one political issue.

I felt guilty driving a cab, and I saw every car and its engine as a small fire that was burning everything up.

But then at some point I sort of just gave up in my mind. I did little things like recycle my plastic bottles and send 10 dollars to Greenpeace, but in my heart, I felt like it was a losing battle.

Man was too destructive, too lost. He would always be at odds with himself and with nature.

It's perhaps too apt a metaphor, but collectively man was like a gigantic alcoholic--he knew better but he couldn't help but destroy himself and everything around him.

My little detective novels were my fantasies--where justice could prevail, though always just barely, and usually at great cost.

So 9/11 confirmed my truest feelings about man--that we were hopelessly imbalanced, that suffering and destruction would always rule.

Ellen was up there alone with her baby. Her life was shattered.

I had no hope for the world, but that doesn't mean I didn't somewhere inside still have hope for my own little life, except all that hope was centered insanely on one person.

THANKS FOR CALLING ME TODAY... I APPRECIATE IT...BYE...YOU DON'T HAVE TO CALL ME BACK...I HOPE YOU'RE ALL RIGHT...I ADORE YOU ...BYE...

As always, I left a message. I tried not to slur my words.

On September 13th, I walked across the Brooklyn Bridge and went to Union Square in Manhattan.

There were no cars south of 14th Street, the city was under martial law. I walked down University Place and saw a huge crowd up ahead.

EXCUSE ME, DO YOU KNOW WHAT'S HAPPENING?

CLINTON IS HERE, HE'S GOING AROUND HUGGING PEOPLE.

Trauma

Analyze

(1) The writer of this graphic novel is Jonathan Ames. The main character in the story is "Jonathan A." What do you make of that? It isn't called an autobiography, but the back cover says there's a "coincidental resemblance" to the author. To what degree are authors connected to every character that they write?

(2) While 9/11 is certainly an emotionally charged event, is it tempered any by your feelings toward a hard-drinking novelist like the main character? Does this character inspire you to root for him or does his self-destructive behavior diminish your sympathy for him?

(3) Haspiel's illustrations are spot-on. He's particularly adept at communicating through body language. Which panel do you think rings the most true? And what's being communicated to the reader purely through the visuals?

(4) How is the setting of this story reflective of Jonathan's life?

Explore

(1) This is a particularly candid look at someone whose life has gone off the rails. How do the visual elements humanize the main character and his struggles?

(2) Can you imagine someone in your community objecting to this text? What would they object to, and why? How would you respond?

(3) In the last panel of this excerpt, Jonathan A. has his head down on the desk after speaking with former president Bill Clinton. What do you imagine is going on in his head?

(4) What do you think will happen after the last panel of this excerpt? Write the next few pages of the story as you imagine it will unfold. Feel free to include your own visuals, too, regardless of your artistic skill level.

MIRIAM ENGELBERG

Cancer Made Me a Shallower Person: A Memoir in Comics

The defining work in Miriam Engelberg's career as a self-taught graphic novelist and illustrator is her memoir, *Cancer Made Me a Shallower Person*, which came about after she was diagnosed with breast cancer at age 43. Instead of wallowing in self-pity, she shares her experience using irreverent and bittersweet humor in her minimal, charming style. Her cartoon *Planet 501c3* was the first cartoon series that—in the office-place satirical style of *Dilbert*—showcased life in the nonprofit world. These cartoons were compiled in two books: *They Came from Planet 501c3* and *Planet 501c3: The Next Generation*. Engelberg's work has also appeared in the *San Francisco Guardian* and *Currents Magazine*.

WORK ABOVE ALL

MY BIOPSY RESULTS WERE DUE BACK ON A MONDAY MORNING. I STARTED THE DAY DOING SOME PREVIOUSLY SCHEDULED WORK ON A CLIENT'S COMPUTER.

FROM THERE I WENT BACK TO THE OFFICE TO WORK ON A COMPUTER MANUAL.

WHEN THE RADIOLOGIST CALLED WITH THE BAD NEWS, I REALIZED HOW FOOLISH I'D BEEN NOT TO TAKE THE DAY OFF.

NOW I NEEDED TO FIGURE OUT THE ETIQUETTE OF CANCER ANNOUNCEMENTS IN THE WORKPLACE.

Miriam Engelberg cordially invites you to join her in reacting to her new CANCER diagnosis. Please—No Gifts.

TWO MONTHS EARLIER A COWORKER HAD BEEN DIAGNOSED WITH CERVICAL CANCER. SHE WAS A CONSULTANT, SO SHE OPTED TO MEET WITH STAFF MEMBERS IN SMALL GROUPS.

I WASN'T THE SMALL GROUP TYPE, SO I DECIDED TO JUST SEND OUT AN E-MAIL.

TO: ALL STAFF
FROM: MIRIAM
SUBJECT: I HAVE BREAST CANCER

ALSO, THE NEW INTRO TO EXCEL MANUAL IS FINISHED.

Trauma

DIAGNOSIS

Trauma

CROSSWORDS

YEARS OF SELF-HELP READING CAME BACK TO ME.

DON'T AVOID—MEDITATE!

THE ONLY WAY OUT IS THROUGH.

HEALING COMES THROUGH FEELING.

THE ANSWER WAS OBVIOUS...

MUST... AVOID... SELF-HELP... PLATITUDES.

JUST AS I WAS READY TO GIVE UP HOPE, I DISCOVERED THE LAST PAGE OF THE SUNDAY PAPER TV GUIDE.

Hmm...

I'D NEVER NOTICED THE TV CROSSWORD PUZZLE BEFORE, BUT NOW I FOUND IT UTTERLY ENCHANTING.

...THE MOTHER ON "HAPPY DAYS"... NOW WHAT WAS HER NAME?

I THOUGHT ABOUT IT ALL THE TIME...

...THEN YOU'LL DO CHEMO, FOLLOWED BY RADIATION.

"LAUGH-IN" REGULAR, 4 LETTERS. LILY? ARTE?

THANKS TO THE CROSSWORD, I REACHED A KIND OF TRIVIA NIRVANA.

CANCER! THAT'S SO AWFUL!

MM HMM...

PRODUCER OF "MELROSE PLACE." I KNOW THAT!

WEIGHT

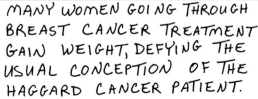

MANY WOMEN GOING THROUGH BREAST CANCER TREATMENT GAIN WEIGHT, DEFYING THE USUAL CONCEPTION OF THE HAGGARD CANCER PATIENT.

I HAVE BREAST CANCER.

SURE YOU DO.

I DIDN'T THINK IT WOULD HAPPEN TO ME. FOR ONE THING, I LOST WEIGHT DURING CHEMO, UNLIKE MANY OF THE WOMEN IN MY GROUP.

I'M TOO NAUSEOUS TO EAT.

REALLY? I'M CONSTANTLY SNACKING.

I'VE GAINED 10 POUNDS!

AND I'D ALWAYS HAD A GOOD METABOLISM.

A SMALL SALAD WITH NO DRESSING.

FETTUCINI ALFREDO WITH EXTRA CREAM.

FOR A FEW MONTHS AFTER FINISHING TREATMENT I REMAINED THIN. THEN SUDDENLY...

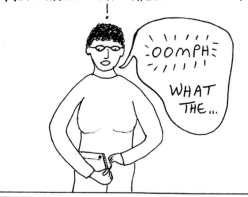

OOMPH

WHAT THE...

WITHOUT CHANGING MY EATING HABITS, I HAD GAINED 15 POUNDS IN TWO MONTHS.

OH MY GOD! HOW DID THIS HAPPEN?

WAS IT THE TAMOXIFEN THAT I HAD TO TAKE FOR 5 YEARS? IT DID COME WITH SOME WARNINGS—

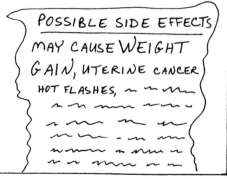

POSSIBLE SIDE EFFECTS

MAY CAUSE WEIGHT GAIN, UTERINE CANCER HOT FLASHES,

Trauma

OR WAS IT FROM SUDDENLY GOING INTO MENOPAUSE COURTESY OF CHEMO?

IT'S LIKE MY META-BOLISM JUST STOPPED.

TELL ME ABOUT IT!

WHATEVER THE CAUSE, THE WEIGHT GAIN WAS ANOTHER IRRITATING REMINDER OF MY BODY'S BETRAYAL.

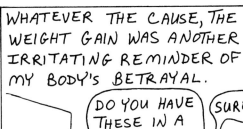

DO YOU HAVE THESE IN A MUCH LARGER SIZE?

SURE!

CHEERFUL BECAUSE IS 16 YEARS OLD WITH TINY → WAIST.

YET, DESPITE ALL THE EVIDENCE, I STILL PICTURED MYSELF AS THE SVELTE PERSON I USED TO BE.

SIZE 4

IT WAS LIKE WHEN I TOOK AEROBICS CLASSES YEARS AGO. WE ALL FACED THE TEACHER AND FOLLOWED HER MOVES.

...AND LIFT AND KICK... YOU'RE DOING GREAT!

WATCHING THE TEACHER I IMAGINED THAT I LOOKED JUST LIKE HER, GRACEFULLY EXECUTING EACH DANCE MOVE.

THEN THE CLASS MOVED TO A ROOM WITH MIRRORS ON ALL THE WALLS,

! OH.

NOW I WAS IN A SIMILAR STATE OF DENIAL ABOUT MY APPEARANCE.

WHO'S THAT PLUMP MIDDLE-AGED WOMAN IN THE WINDOW?

BUT THEN AGAIN, I'VE NEVER COMPLETELY ACCEPTED ADULTHOOD. IN MY MIND I'M STUCK SOMEWHERE IN MY 20s.

THIS "FELICITY" EPISODE IS RIVETING! WILL SHE GO FOR PRE-MED OR SWITCH TO ART?

INWARDLY, I'M STILL THE SAME PERSON I WAS 25 YEARS AGO.

THIS PHILOSOPHY CLASS IS CHANGING MY LIFE!

SO TRUE!

KANT

KANT

OR IS THAT JUST ANOTHER MISPERCEPTION?

THIS PHILOSOPHY CLASS IS CHANGING MY LIFE!

I DOUBT IT.

KANT

TV GUIDE

LUCKILY, CARTOONING FORCES ME TO GET HONEST ABOUT WHO I REALLY AM.

OVER 5' TALL

ONLY HAS KIND THOUGHTS ABOUT OTHERS.

I HAVE A DUTY TO PORTRAY MYSELF AS REALISTICALLY AS POSSIBLE!

TINY WAIST

NEVER CHOOSES "PEOPLE" MAGAZINE OVER "THE NEW YORKER".

END

Trauma

AS I GRADUALLY RECOVERED FROM THE DEBILITATING EFFECTS OF CHEMO AND RADIATION, I REALIZED SOMETHING WAS MISSING... BUT WHAT?

HMM...MY HAIR'S COMING BACK, MY APPETITE'S BACK, MY BRAIN'S SORT OF BACK...

HONEY—ARE YOU COMING TO BED? I'M NAKED AND WAITING...

NO—I'M TRYING TO REMEMBER SOMETHING, AND THEN I'M GOING TO WATCH MANY HOURS OF LATE NIGHT TV.

HOLD ON...THAT'S IT! I'M MISSING MY LIBIDO!

IT'S NOT SURPRISING, REALLY. CHEMO PUT ME INTO SUDDEN MENOPAUSE, AND MEDICATION CONTINUED THE JOB OF SUPPRESSING ANY ESTROGEN THAT WAS LEFT.

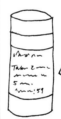

TAKE 2 TABLETS BEFORE BEDTIME FOR 5 YEARS. REFILLS LEFT: 59

AT FIRST I EMBRACED MY NEW STATE.

I'M SO MUCH HAPPIER NOW. NO MIGRAINES, NO PMS MOOD SWINGS... IT'S GREAT!

YOUR ATTITUDE IS SO INSPIRING.

I WATCHED ROMANTIC SCENES IN MOVIES FROM A DETACHED, ANTHROPOLOGICAL PERSPECTIVE.

FASCINATING— THESE HOMO SAPIENS EVIDENTLY GET PLEASURE FROM THE APPLICATION OF ONE SET OF LIPS OVER ANOTHER.

Ooh...
mmm...
ahh...
slurp...

Trauma

WE INTERRUPT THESE PHILOSOPHICAL MUSINGS WITH AN INVITATION TO HAWAII...

FORMER CO-WORKER, NOW A PROPERTY MANAGER ON MAUI.

...AND THE OWNERS SAID YOU CAN STAY IN THE GUESTHOUSE.

I LEFT JIM AND AARON AT HOME AND SET OFF FOR A RESTFUL WEEK IN HAWAII. IN BETWEEN SWIMMING AND READING TRASH BOOKS BY THE POOL, I WATCHED CABLE TV IN MY ROOM.

NOW THAT YOU'VE OVERCOME BULIMIA AND A DRUG HABIT YOU CAN FOCUS ON TRAPPING THAT STALKER!

HMM, I THINK I'VE SEEN THIS LIFETIME MOVIE ALREADY. OR DID I?

YES, BUT FIRST I NEED TO PROVE THAT MY HUSBAND POISONED HIS FIRST WIFE.

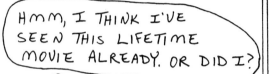

I'D BEEN WONDERING FOR AWHILE WHETHER WATCHING PORN COULD JUMP-START MY LIBIDO. THE CABLE GUIDE LISTED AN ADULT CHANNEL, SO I GAVE IT A TRY.

AWW MAN— IT'S SCRAMBLED!

STILL, A LITTLE OF THE MOVIE MADE IT THROUGH.

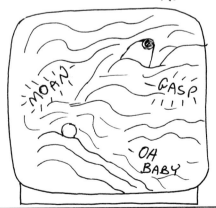

MOAN

GASP

OH BABY

I HAD TO ADMIT IT WAS A TURN-ON, INTERMITTENTLY...

WHOA — LOOK AT THE SIZE OF... OH WAIT, THAT'S JUST AN ARM.

WHEN I GOT BACK TO SAN FRANCISCO I DECIDED TO RENT AN EROTIC MOVIE. I PICKED A QUIET TIME AT MY LOCAL VIDEO STORE AND PUSHED THE SWINGING RED DOORS INTO THE ADULT AREA.

BEING IN A ROOM FILLED WITH PORN WAS OVERWHELMING, ESPECIALLY WHEN ALL THE MOVIES SEEMED AIMED AT MEN...

BREAST-ENHANCED VIXENS WITH GUYS LIKE YOU

WHEN A MAN CAME INTO THE AREA, I HURRIEDLY LEFT. THAT'S WHEN I SPOTTED A SOFT-CORE SECTION OUT IN THE REGULAR STORE.

HMM— "EMMANUELLE"!

"EMMANUELLE" WAS A CLASSIC—WHEN I WAS IN COLLEGE IT PLAYED AT THE UNIVERSITY CINEMA. SOME GUYS FROM MY DORM WENT TO SEE IT AND CAME BACK SEMI-TRAUMATIZED.

IT WAS INTENSE!

IT FREAKED ME OUT, MAN.

BUT WHEN JIM AND I STARTED WATCHING, WE GOT BORED PRETTY QUICKLY. FOR ONE THING, THERE WAS A LOT OF DUBBED 1970s-STYLE DIALOGUE...

YOU ARE NOT MY PLAYTHING AND YOU ARE NOT MY BEAUTY— YOU ARE BEAUTY.

CAN THIS... BE LOVE?

...AND THE SEX SCENES ALL ENDED JUST AS THINGS WERE GETTING INTERESTING...

LET'S FAST-FORWARD TO A SEX SCENE.

THIS IS A SEX SCENE.

SEX

THAT'S WHEN I STARTED WONDERING...

SINCE I NO LONGER WANT SEX, WHY AM I TRYING SO HARD TO WANT IT AGAIN?

THE THING IS, THERE'S SOMETHING DRAB ABOUT A LIFE WITHOUT SEXUAL DESIRE—EVERYTHING GOES A LITTLE FLAT. IT'S KIND OF LIKE THE END OF A LOVE AFFAIR.

LIFE AND I USED TO BE INVOLVED, BUT NOW WE'RE JUST FRIENDS.

THE BEGINNING OF THE RELATIONSHIP WAS GREAT—I WAS INFATUATED BY EVERY LITTLE THING LIFE HAD TO OFFER.

WOW—LIGHT!!!

-COO-
-CHORTLE

LATER ON IT TOOK MORE TO KEEP THE SPARK ALIVE.

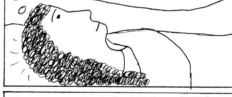

MY LIFE IS SO DULL. I KNOW! I'LL WRITE A NOVEL, LEARN RUSSIAN AND PERFORM STAND-UP COMEDY.

BUT EVENTUALLY LIFE AND I REACHED A LOW POINT.

IT'S NOT YOU—IT'S ME. I JUST DON'T FIND YOU EXCITING ANYMORE.

I HAVEN'T GIVEN UP, THOUGH. I'M JUST SEARCHING FOR THE RIGHT KIND OF PORN.

YEAH, BABY—WRITE THAT NOVEL! OH YEAH... IT'S HAUNTING AND LUMINOUS... AND REALLY LONG...

END

Analyze

(1) Unlike the illustration style of many of the artists in this book, Engelberg's doesn't rely on classical skills of draftsmanship. In fact, it might best be described as scribbly. How does her pen-and-ink stylistic choice affect this work? Does it impact the tone, meaning, or humor of this subject? How so? Consider comparing Engelberg's style to that of Lynda Barry and Mary Fleener, two talented illustrators who sometimes adopt an anti-classical mode.

(2) In graphic narratives, spoken dialogue is conveyed by enclosing words within a balloon that tapers to a point near a character's mouth. Thought is conveyed by enclosing words within a balloon that is accompanied by progressively smaller, empty balloons culminating near a character's mouth or head. What are the other words you see that aren't in any balloons? Look at the first few pages of this excerpt. What distinction do you make between those other words and the words within any type of balloon? Why make that visual distinction? Is there a hierarchy in play?

(3) Engelberg realizes that, try as she might, she can't jumpstart her libido. "The thing is," says the one panel, "there's something drab about a life without sexual desire—everything—goes a little flat. It's kind of like the end of a love affair." And to emphasize the point, she actually says, "Life and I used to be involved, but now we're just friends." How important is a sexual life to her, really? Is this yearning primarily about sex, or is it suggestive of something else—such as desire, self-worth, emotional expansiveness?

Explore

(1) In a 2006 interview, Engelberg said, "Somehow in the cartoon form, panel by panel, the absurdist part of this whole experience comes out in a way that it wouldn't if I were just writing an essay." In what way does a graphic narrative allow for meaning that a text-only essay does not? How can the visual presence of a cartoon—and the spaces between panels—create a unique space for personal revelation?

(2) In Michael Chaney's TedxDartmouth Talk "How to Read a Graphic Novel," readily found online, he says that graphic narratives offer us the keen ability to see an individual within the context of the social. The interplay of text plus images allows us to see abstractions more readily. What abstractions do you notice in Engelberg's comic? What meanings occur in this comic because of the relationship of the individual and the social?

(3) Humor plays a large part in this story. What parts did you find funny? Did you feel awkward laughing while reading a story about cancer? Listen to the NPR interview "Miriam Engelberg, Cartoonist Who Conquered Cancer," in which she talks about using humor in this text (*All Things Considered*, October 18, 2006). To hear more from her, also consider listening to "Chronicling Cancer, in Graphic Form" (*All Things Considered*, June 29, 2006).

History

For decades now, graphic authors have created historically based works that incorporate verbal texts and engaging visuals to draw in readers to stories based firmly in key moments of human history. Many graphic authors rely on archival research, oral histories, and first-person accounts to solidify the historical details presented in their work. Well-known examples of this visual genre include *J. Edgar Hoover: A Graphic Biography* (about Hoover's rise within the FBI as much as a history of the agency) and *Bluesman: A Twelve Bar Graphic Narrative in the Key of Life and Death* (a three-part series about the Great Depression and the Deep South).

Our own choices for this section follow in this goal of presenting narratives of history that combine verbal and visual elements. "A Short History of America" by Robert Crumb does exactly what one would think, by allowing images to communicate one perspective on U.S. history. *March*, by Congressman John Lewis, Andrew Aydin, and Nate Powell, offers up a vivid personal account of a key figure in the American civil rights movement by adapting the congressman's life story into visual form. The excerpt from Derf's *My Friend Dahmer* presents a sympathetic perspective of one of the most notorious serial killers in the last century, Jeffrey Dahmer. Another complex period in history—the making of the atomic bomb and the Manhattan Project—is explored in "Trinity" by Michael Cho. *Annie Sullivan and the Trials of Helen Keller* by Joseph Lambert showcases the teacher-student relationship between Annie Sullivan and Helen Keller, a relationship in which both people struggled to overcome severe disabilities. Finally, Liana Finck's *A Bintel Brief: Love and Longing in Old New York* delves into the immigrant experience in New York City at the start of the twentieth century.

Other texts in this book could easily enter into a discussion of visual history. For instance, Marjane Satrapi's *Persepolis* offers insight into religious persecution in the 1970s. Art Spiegelman's "In the Shadow of No Towers" reflects on one of the most important historical moments in America in the last few decades.

Simply put, historical narratives are the means by which many people understand present issues of culture, politics, and identity. Visual authors attempt to deliver the past—word by word, image by image—to their readers. These stories serve as windows on to a reconstructed past, an immersive art that combines research and narrative skill. But like works of narrative nonfiction or general history, these visual works often contain an argument, a point of view that the author wants to explore or deliver through a story. Nowhere in this book is that more apparent than in this section—where graphic authors draw from their own experiences (memoir) or create invented situations (fiction) to apply their craft to historical subjects.

As the chapter unfolds, consider how visual texts connect readers to historical experience in ways that differ from those of traditional verbal texts. Also, practice active reading by noticing how history—of all forms—is often a personal narrative, in which an author frames the importance of each event (emphasizing some details in large panels, omitting others), arranges the episode to tell a story, and quite often delivers a message.

ROBERT CRUMB

"A Short History of America"

Considered a founder of the 1960s underground comix movement following his *Zap Comix* publication in 1963, counterculture cartoonist Robert Crumb—often referred to as R. Crumb—regularly satirizes the foibles and excesses of American culture. Crumb is known for creating memorable characters such as Mr. Natural and Fritz the Cat. A good deal of his own work appeared in *Weirdo*, a magazine he founded in 1981 that ran for twelve years. In 1991, Crumb was inducted into Will Eisner's Comic Book Hall of Fame.

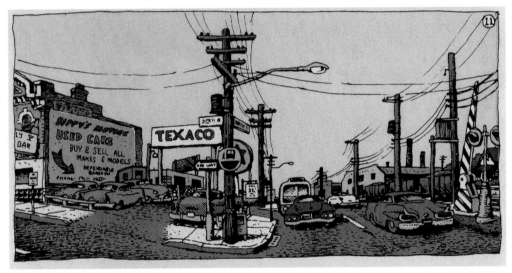

History

Analyze

(1) Many graphic narratives alter the drawing's perspective (visual point of view) for a variety of reasons, all of which have to do with conveying meaning. Crumb's story, however, uses a fixed perspective. Why do you think this is so? What meaning(s) does this give access to that a changing perspective might not as easily allow?

(2) Other than "A Short History of America" at the start and a few words in the last panels, this is a story without captions or dialogue. Why is that an interesting choice? Could you write a story to accompany the images? What might be lost if readers had only your story version but not the images?

(3) If you take "A Short History of America" as an argument, what is its thesis? Its evidence? Are there any cause-and-effect relationships shown? What is its conclusion?

(4) How does Crumb show the passage of time? What elements does he include to help readers identify each era?

Explore

(1) The version of "A Short History of America" here is colored, though it originally appeared as a black-and-white graphic narrative in *Co-Evolutionary Quarterly* in 1979. In 1981, it was rearranged and colored by Peter Poplaski to be sold as a poster. Find an image of the original black-and-white version online. How does color add or detract? What do you think about colorizing a black-and-white graphic narrative? A film? Does it change the meaning or simply add visual appeal?

(2) In 1560, Flemish artist Pieter Bruegel the Elder painted "Children's Games," which showed dozens upon dozens of children playing in a village square. View a copy of it online. It's unrealistic to imagine all of those children playing there at the same time. But if you view the same scene on a number of different days, you might indeed have an accumulation of images that equals the boisterousness of Bruegel's single scene. How does this strategy of accumulation inform your reading of "A Short History of America"? What films, music, or other artworks can you think of that utilize a similar method of accumulation to create meaning?

(3) What do you think your own neighborhood will look like in twenty-five years? Draw it. Or describe it in clear, specific, vivid language.

JOSEPH LAMBERT

Annie Sullivan and the Trials of Helen Keller

The illustrations of Joseph Lambert, a graduate of the Center for Cartoon Studies, have appeared in *Popular Mechanics*, *The Comics Journal*, *Business Week*, and many other publications. His debut graphic novel, *I Will Bite You!* won the 2011 Ignatz Award for Outstanding Collection and Outstanding Artist. His follow up, *Annie Sullivan and the Trials of Helen Keller*, won the 2013 Eisner Award for Best Reality-Based Work.

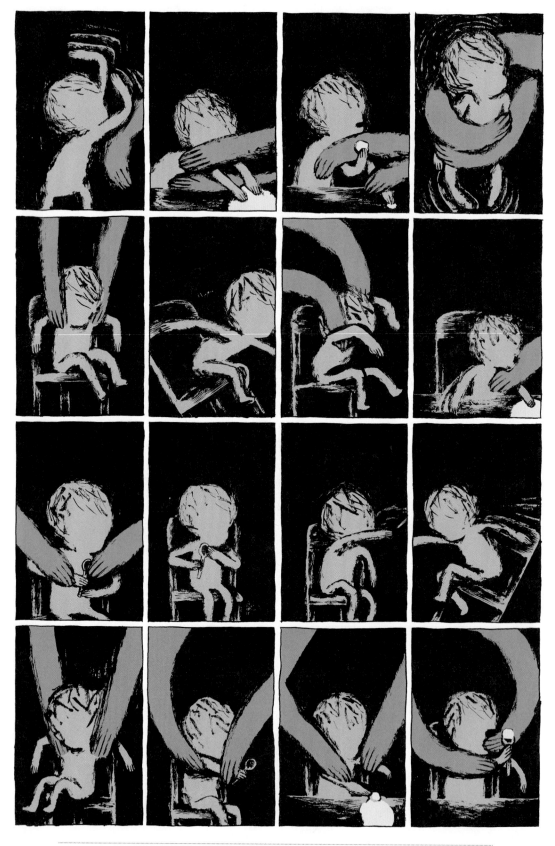

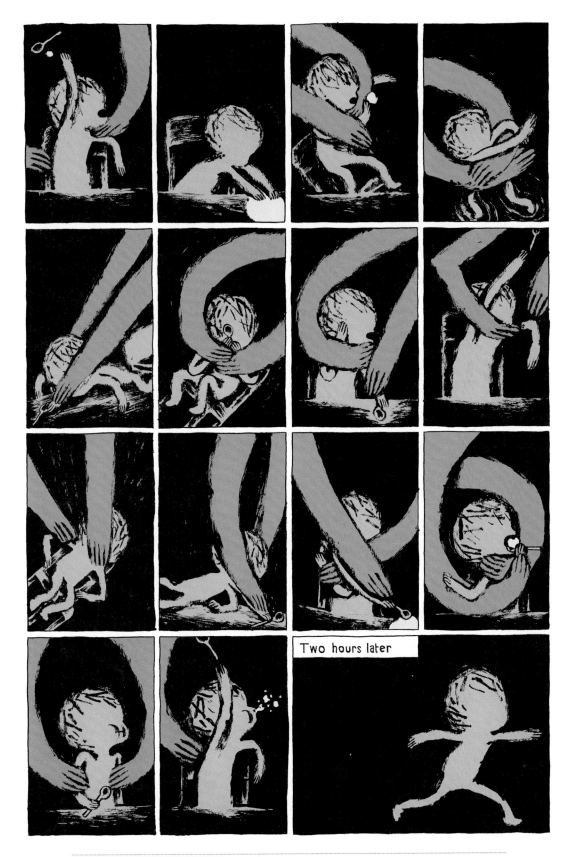

Two hours later

History

Boston, Massachusetts
5 days before

Your ticket, Annie.

Thank you, Mr. Anagnos. I'll pay you back as soon as I set up a bank account in Alabama.

Please,

consider it a gift.

And speaking of gifts...

Laura stitched the dress. From one deaf-blind girl to another. Glorious, yes?!

It... it's lovely. Helen will love it.

Yes. I'm sure she will.

Now, you should put your glasses on. We don't want you undoing your recent surgery.

Annie...

I'm fine.

I often forget how young you are.

Years before

You are fourteen years old and you can't spell your own name?! I've never heard of such a thing!

I'm sure there is much you have not heard of.

:gasp:

:gasp:

Heh.

Expel her?!

Expel her to where? She has no place to go!

Where do you go when you die?

Well, I— :ahem: You—

I know! The Deep!

Annie, I have told you before to wait until you are called upon to speak—

You go to the Deep when you die.

:Sigh:

The what?

The Deep. When you die, you sink into the ocean and you're rocked like a baby—

Annie—

And it's cold and dark...

Where did you hear such a story?!

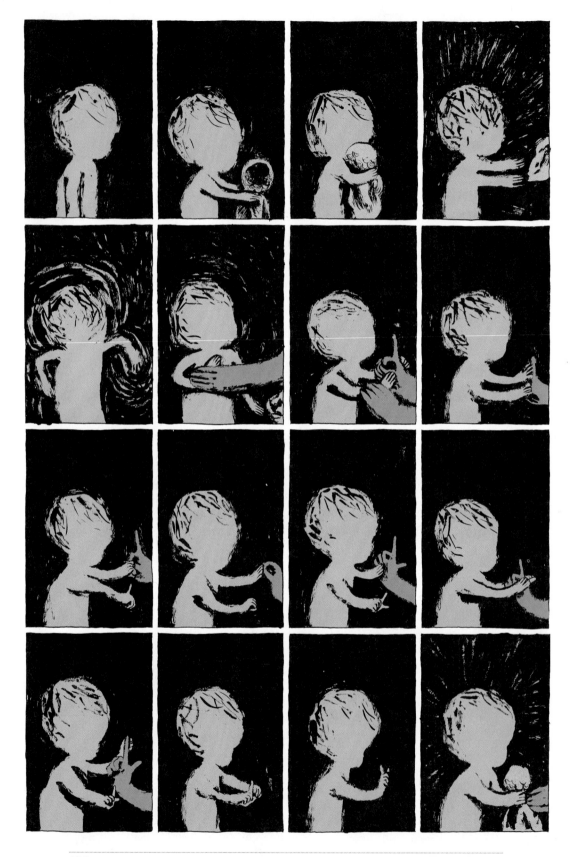

History

History

History

Analyze

(1) The panels with a black background present the way Helen Keller might have experienced the world. How is the visual presentation of the "Keller" panels unique? Consider use of color, definition of line, use or absence of language, arrangement of shapes, use of nonvisual sensory details, and so on.

(2) The story of Helen Keller and Annie Sullivan highlights the barriers people with severe disabilities confront on a daily basis, but it also explores the role of a dedicated teacher. Annie Sullivan says that she accepts the job with the Kellers because she needs the paycheck, yet her determination with Helen Keller far exceeds the role of tutor. Explain Annie Sullivan's motivation to work as a teacher despite the obvious difficulties and hardships.

(3) Early in the story, Annie Sullivan explains that the "battle" was necessary. The idea of "battling" or "restraining a student's will through force" has long fallen out of popularity in models of Western education. Why is it effective here?

(4) In popular culture, the terms "hero" and "celebrity" are often confused. Annie Sullivan, through strict lessons and years of perseverance, expands Helen Keller's vocabulary to include hundreds of words. Sullivan teaches Keller to explore math and to memorize multiplication tables. Sullivan would later become famous for her work and lifelong friendship with Helen Keller. Sullivan's story is presented not only in this comic, but also in *The Miracle Worker*, originally a TV drama and later a successful play on Broadway. In your opinion, is Annie Sullivan more of a hero or a celebrity? Use the Internet to better understand the life of Annie Sullivan.

Explore

(1) One of the concepts that Annie Sullivan eventually teaches Helen, who has been blind since the age of two, is the idea of color. In three well-developed paragraphs, present an explanation of color—what it is, how it affects people, its various purposes—using language that could be understood by a person born without sight.

(2) The comic contrasts Annie Sullivan's disciplinary teaching style with Helen's father's nurturing and mollifying parenting style. In your opinion, which is more beneficial for Helen? For children in general?

(3) Using a color medium (pens, pencils, pastels, crayons, photography, etc.), create an image that explains music to someone who cannot hear. How can visual language be used to express music, an abstract concept, to someone who cannot experience it directly?

(4) As an adult, Annie Sullivan struggled with language—spelling in particular. Yet she so believed in the importance of language that she taught Helen Keller to identify objects by name, thereby bringing her into verbal experience. In an essay, describe an experience in which you learned a difficult skill (drawing, dance, woodwork, calculus, etc.) even though you did not have an initial, natural ability with it. What drew you to the experience, and what motivated you to persevere? In what ways did you succeed?

LIANA FINCK

A Bintel Brief: Love and Longing in Old New York

While Liana Finck's parents both grew up as Orthodox Jews, she moved away from religion when she studied at Cooper Union art school in Manhattan. Afterward, during a year in Belgium on a Fulbright Scholarship, she began creating a comic book based on the life of the Belgian comic artist Georges Remi, famous for his *Tintin* series. Although she didn't finish that book, she did return to New York, where she wrote *A Bintel Brief* to try to recapture an appreciation for Judaism. Finck has also published in *The Forward* newspaper and *Tablet Magazine*.

THE NIGHT OF THE POGROM I WAS READING OUTSIDE, SO I SAW THEM COMING.

I RAN WITHOUT KNOWING WHAT I WAS DOING.

THAT'S HOW I ESCAPED. ALONE.

I NEVER SAW MY FAMILY AGAIN.

I CAN'T STOP THINKING ABOUT MY FATHER.

My God.

MY SISTERS TELL ME HE LAY UNCONSCIOUS FOR FOUR DAYS. THEY TENDED TO HIS WOUND.

HE AWOKE IN THE MIDDLE OF THE FOURTH NIGHT. CRAZED WITH GRIEF AND FEVER, HE WANDERED OFF.

Oh, my God.

I KNOW MY FATHER BETTER THAN ANYONE. I KNOW WHAT HE THINKS ABOUT ON A CLEAR NIGHT.

HE RECALLS THE PASSAGE IN THE TORAH WHERE GOD TELLS ABRAHAM HE WILL HAVE AS MANY DESCENDANTS AS THERE ARE STARS IN THE SKY.

MY FATHER STILL BELIEVES THIS. THAT IS THE REAL MIRACLE.

Brooklyn, New York.
1906

NOBODY HERE SEEMS AWARE OF THE BETRAYED SHTETL GHOSTS THAT FOLLOW ME AROUND —

LETTER FOR YA.

THANK YOU.

WHISPERING THAT THIS IS NOT MY PLACE,

THAT AT ANY MOMENT AMERICA WILL FALL AWAY —

AND I'LL BE HOME AGAIN.

MY SISTERS WROTE TO ME:

Analyze

(1) Using the Internet, learn about the pogroms in Russia (1903–1906) that left thousands of Jews homeless or dead. How does historical information about the pogroms deepen or change your understanding of this comic?

(2) The visual style of this comic alludes to elements that defined early printing: some panels contain halftones, others feature relief printing such as woodcut, and still others suggest the high contrast of early photography. How do these visual elements contribute to the meaning and "feel" of the comic?

(3) The "father" in this story lives in a region of ethnic and religious persecution. The violence against Jews is so severe that many are killed. Why can't the narrator, Yekheil, imagine his father leaving the brutality of Russia to find a new life in America?

(4) The writer of the letter seeks advice. His sisters have enough money to come to America—also to bring their father with them—but it's clear that the move would likely devastate the father in that he would lose his home culture. If you were to answer his letter, how would you respond: would you advise Yekheil to bring the rest of his family, including his father, to America?

Explore

(1) "A Bintel Brief" (Yiddish for "a bundle of letters") was originally an advice column for a widely read Yiddish newspaper in New York at the start of the 1900s. In what way does Finck's visual adaptation of this letter serve as a type of advice for contemporary readers? What can contemporary readers learn from correspondence written over a century ago?

(2) In this comic, the narrator seeks refuge in America to escape religious persecution. In a class discussion, explore the reasons people now seek to immigrate to America.

(3) This Bintel Brief explores the difficulty of leaving one culture to assimilate into another. With members of your class, create a list of elements of American life that you would most miss if you moved to another country. Consider freedoms, education, popular culture, the familiarity of your home state, cuisine, national history, fashion, and friendships.

(4) This comic explores a father's disappointment when his son, Yekheil, leaves Russia—and the Jewish culture of the shtetl—to find a new life in Brooklyn, New York. In an essay, explore two or three core values of your family so central to life at home that your parents would be disappointed if you abandoned them. What is it about these core values that contributes to your family identity?

JOHN LEWIS, ANDREW AYDIN, AND NATE POWELL

March

Since 1987, John Lewis has served as the U.S. Representative for Georgia's Fifth Congressional District. Born in Troy, Alabama, Lewis became the youngest of the "Big Six" civil rights leaders during the 1960s. *March* is a black-and-white graphic novel trilogy that tells the story of the U.S. civil rights movement through Lewis's eyes.

A graduate of Trinity College and Georgetown University, Andrew Aydin is a politician who serves as telecommunications and technology policy aide to Congressman John Lewis. Together, they cowrote *March*.

Nate Powell, a graphic novelist and musician, began self-publishing comics in his teens before majoring in cartooning at the School of the Visual Arts in New York City. For the next decade, he worked as a caregiver for adults with developmental disabilities and also ran the punk record label DIY as well as performed in punk bands such as WAIT, Soophie Nun Squad, and Divorce Chord. His 2008 graphic novel, *Swallow Me Whole*, was a finalist for the *Los Angeles Times Book Prize* in the Young Adult category. He provided the illustrations for *March*.

THE THING IS, WHEN I WAS YOUNG, THERE **WASN'T** MUCH OF A CIVIL RIGHTS MOVEMENT. I WANTED TO WORK AT **SOMETHING**, BUT GROWING UP IN RURAL ALABAMA, MY PARENTS KNEW IT COULD BE **DANGEROUS** TO MAKE ANY WAVES.

stay out of trouble.

don't get in white people's way.

BUT OTHER MEMBERS OF MY FAMILY HELPED OPEN MY EYES.

IN THE SUMMER OF 1951, I TOOK MY FIRST TRIP NORTH.

OTIS CARTER, ONE OF MY MOTHER'S BROTHERS, ARRANGED THE JOURNEY. HE PLANNED IT COMPLETELY FOR MY SAKE.

HE LIVED IN DOTHAN, ABOUT SIXTY MILES SOUTH OF US, WHERE HE WAS A TEACHER AND A SCHOOL PRINCIPAL.

THERE WOULD BE NO RESTAURANTS FOR US TO STOP AT UNTIL WE WERE **WELL** OUT OF THE SOUTH,

SO WE CARRIED OUR RESTAURANT RIGHT IN THE CAR WITH US.

STOPPING FOR GAS AND BATHROOM BREAKS TOOK CAREFUL PLANNING. UNCLE OTIS HAD MADE THIS TRIP BEFORE, AND HE KNEW WHICH PLACES ALONG THE WAY OFFERED "COLORED" BATHROOMS--

AND WHICH WERE SAFER TO JUST PASS ON BY.

ALABAMA.

TENNESSEE.

KENTUCKY.

THESE WERE THE STATES WE
HAD TO BE CAREFUL IN AS WE
MADE OUR WAY NORTH.

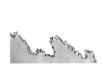

History

BLACK DRIVERS WE PASSED GOING THE OTHER DIRECTION,
FROM NORTH TO SOUTH,
FACED AN ADDED DANGER, THEIR LICENSE PLATES MAKING THEM VISIBLE TARGETS.
NEW YORK
14TTZ
SOMETIMES THEY HAD TO FACE WORSE.
what are them yankee niggers doing with a car like that?

MY AUNT LEOLA AND AUNT MAE CHARLES TOOK ME SHOPPING DOWNTOWN ONE DAY AT A DEPARTMENT STORE CALLED SATTLER'S.

THERE, FOR THE FIRST TIME IN MY LIFE, I RODE AN ESCALATOR.

I HAD NEVER EVEN HEARD OF SUCH A THING.

I FOUND MY WAY TO THE CANDY COUNTER AND IT WAS LIKE MAGIC.

I TRIED TO MAKE THAT BAG OF NEAPOLITAN CANDY LAST FOREVER.

ANOTHER TIME, WE WENT TO THE OUTDOOR MARKET AND I WATCHED MY AUNT LEOLA SHOP FOR A CHICKEN.

CITY PEOPLE DIDN'T RAISE THEIR OWN CHICKENS. THEY DID WHAT MY AUNT DID--

I WANT THAT ONE.

THAT AMAZED ME. IT WAS SO DIFFERENT FROM BACK HOME.

I WASN'T EVEN BOTHERED BY THE FATE OF THESE CHICKENS.

MAYBE THE FACT THAT I DIDN'T KNOW THEM HAD SOMETHING TO DO WITH IT. I DON'T KNOW.

I DO KNOW THAT I HAD NO PROBLEM CLEANING MY PLATE THAT EVENING.

BY LATE AUGUST WHEN IT WAS TIME TO RETURN TO ALABAMA, I WAS MORE THAN READY.

I MISSED MY BROTHERS AND SISTERS.

I MISSED MY PARENTS.

WHEN I FINALLY ARRIVED HOME, I WAS CRYING BECAUSE IT FELT SO GOOD TO BE BACK.

Thank you, uncle otis.

Analyze

(1) Using the Internet, develop a list of common social injustices faced by African-Americans in the South prior to the passage of the Civil Rights Act of 1964. Consider segregation in restaurants and other public spaces, use of public transportation, access to schools, ability to register to vote, segregation in the military and sports, and so on. How does the experience of John Lewis, as depicted in this comic, represent aspects of the pre–civil rights African-American experience that you discovered through your Internet research?

(2) How do the drawings of Buffalo, New York, convey a different social experience compared with those of rural Alabama? Notice facial expressions, bodily gesture, the use of light, the size and shape of panels, and so on.

(3) How does John Lewis's experience in the North differ from his experience in Alabama? Consider technology, social and cultural freedom, racial integration, availability of food, racial concerns, ease of transportation, availability of services (such as restaurants), and availability of services such as restaurants.

(4) In the final panel, John Lewis makes reference to "riding the bus to school, which should've been fun." From a historical perspective, what is the importance of this bus ride?

Explore

(1) Using the Internet, learn about the life of John Lewis, a congressperson representing Georgia's Fifth District. How do you think his early experiences, as represented in this comic, helped give rise to his later accomplishments?

(2) Using the NAACP website (http://www.naacp.org/), explore contemporary issues of civil rights and social justice. How might contemporary concerns of racial equality/inequality be related to the experiences depicted in this comic?

(3) John Lewis explains that after his trip north, "home never felt the same." Using both text and drawings, create a short comic in which you present an experience that changed the way you felt about "home."

(4) John Lewis's autobiographical comic explores the social injustices of the early 1950s. In an essay, explore what you believe is the most significant social injustice of the current day. Your essay might touch on an issue of sexual orientation, disabilities, political influence, ethnicity, religion, class, wealth, education, or the environment. Be sure to address how this issue has affected your own life or the life of someone you know.

MICHAEL CHO

"Trinity"

Michael Cho was born in South Korea but moved to Canada at age six. Cho says he's an "illustrator, cartoonist, and occasional writer based in Toronto." He's the author of an art book, *Back Alleys and Urban Landscapes*, as well as the graphic novel *Shoplifter*. Cho has also provided cover and story illustrations for *Batman Black and White*, *Age of the Sentry*, and *X-Men First Class*.

Maybe it's less relevant now. Certainly the 21st century has brought on newer horrors and a fresher batch of difficult questions.

But to me, the world I was born into and grew up in began here, in this place, and on this date:

July 16th, 1945.

Here, at 5:29 am, the effort of 6000 men and women came to its conclusion.

In a flash brighter than a thousand suns...

...and with the echo of thunder across the desert hills.

trinity

History

December, 1938: fission is discovered by scientists in Germany, splitting the atom and unleashing undreamt of amounts of energy. As the news spreads around the world, top physicists immediately grasp the possibility of creating an atomic bomb.

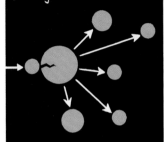

August, 1939: fearing that Nazi scientists may already be working on it, Leo Szilard convinces Albert Einstein to write to President Roosevelt, urging the start of an American-led atomic project.

December, 1941: Pearl Harbor plunges the U.S. into World War II, and the bomb program picks up momentum. Now code named the Manhattan Project, it's headed by General Leslie Groves; the man who built the Pentagon.

At a top secret complex built on the grounds of a former boys school in Los Alamos, New Mexico, the best and brightest scientific minds of the free world are assembled for the task.

Among them:

Hans Bethe: principal theoretician, driven to join in an effort to stop the Nazis.

Niels Bohr: "the Great Dane", Nobel Prize winner and father figure to many of the assembled.

Enrico Fermi: chief experimentalist, who works on the atomic chain reaction.

Ernest O. Lawrence: inventor of the cyclotron, which produces fissionable material.

Edward Teller: the physicist who advocates the construction of a hydrogen "super" bomb.

And overseeing them all, J. Robert Oppenheimer, chief physicist and director of operations.

Oppenheimer is an odd choice to head the massive project.

Elegant and urbane, he speaks 6 languages and loves 16th century poetry. Before choosing physics, he considered becoming an architect or a poet.

A child prodigy, he graduated Harvard in 3 years, summa cum laude, and was awarded a rare dual professorship at Berkeley and Caltech by the age of 25.

Even from youth, he seems a man headed for a special destiny. His brother describes him as someone who needed to make everything he did seem special.

He was the kind of person who, "If he went off in the woods to take a leak, he'd come back with a flower."

Though unconcerned with current events in his early life, the rise of Hitler and fascism in Europe awakens his political side.

On a train ride from Berkeley to New York, he reads all 3 volumes of Marx's "Das Kapital" in the original German text.

The Manhattan Project gives Oppenheimer the opportunity to use his intellect in the fight against fascism. It also presents what he calls a "technically sweet" problem.

It's an irresistable lure to the scientist - to transform ideas and theories into a working physical device. In hindsight, it's a classic Faustian bargain.

The U.S. Army gave him unlimited resources and Oppenheimer would sell a part of his soul for the chance to unlock and control the basic power of the universe.

At Los Alamos, the impractical lover of meta-physical poetry quickly transforms himself into the perfect administrator. The walled town is a strange, hastily built place, where liberal scientists mix with Army G.I.s.

The list of local attractions is unique: 2 dance bands, 1 soda fountain, boys and girls scout clubs, 1 cyclotron and 7000 fire extinguishers.

Equally unique is the egalitarian makeup of the scientific community. The senior scientists bring their brightest students and their families. There are no class distinctions. Nobel laureates and precocious protéges are all united in one purpose: to beat the Nazis in the race to build the first atomic bomb.

camping trip

Metallurgy

baseball Fri

Fermi

soon to wed?

Kitty & Oppie

chemist club

For the professors used to Ivy League corridors and comforts, it's a big change to walk muddy streets and huddle in parkas around coal stoves. There are only 5 bathtubs and water is in short supply. Once, when the taps run dry, they are issued a memo to brush their teeth with Coca-Cola.

For the young, the project is a grand adventure. They work around the clock, but hold many parties. Alcohol is scarce, so they make do with punch spiked with 200 proof lab alcohol.

For many, it must have seemed the best time of their lives.

From 1941 to 1945, as men die by the thousands across Europe and the Pacific, development on the bomb proceeds at a feverish pace. By 1944, Los Alamos has a population of 6000 scientists and staff.

The lab complex has 7 divisions:

THEORETICAL PHYSICS
CHEMISTRY
ORDINANCE
EXPLOSIVES
BOMB PHYSICS
EXPERIMENTAL PHYSICS
METALLURGY

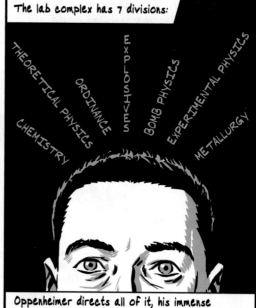

Oppenheimer directs all of it, his immense intelligence encompassing all the minute details of every department.

With the inclusion of 2 giant plants elsewhere in the U.S. for the production of plutonium and uranium, the Manhattan Project becomes the single most expensive scientific project of all time. The total cost: over 2 billion dollars.

Finally, in March 1945, allied troops enter Germany, on the home stretch to victory in Europe. Soldiers begin raiding bombed out labs, and Army intelligence sees for itself the state of the Nazi atomic program.

The news comes quickly to Los Alamos.

There is no Nazi bomb.

The Germans weren't even close to completing it.

Now the scientists of the Manhattan Project are at a crossroads.

Should they stop work on the bomb? There's no chance that Japan can build one.

Or should they continue and finish building the most destructive weapon in human history?

End of Part One

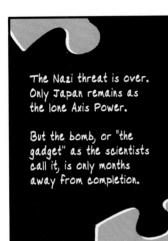

The Nazi threat is over. Only Japan remains as the lone Axis Power.

But the bomb, or "the gadget" as the scientists call it, is only months away from completion.

In the years to come, many of them would wonder why they didn't just stop and walk away from the project after Germany's defeat. Some would agonize over it.

But right now, it's just not in the air.

For over 4 years, the men and women at Los Alamos have been consumed by their work.

And they're so close now, so close to unlocking the puzzle.

The machinery of war is also still in motion.

There are sailors and ships waiting to transport the finished bomb.

Island airbases are being built in the Pacific to launch the raids against Japan.

And bomber crews are training in the U.S. to deliver the world's first atomic strike.

Against all this, it would take a monumental effort of will to stop the project.

In the end, only a token meeting is organized by the scientists.

Less than 50 people attend.

MEETING TODAY: "THE IMPACT OF THE GADGET ON CIVILIZATION"

SENIOR STAFF

Oppenheimer is among them.

At the meeting, some suggest that it's time to abandon the effort. That it would be morally wrong to continue.

Oppenheimer argues otherwise.

The bomb is a weapon so terrible, it can make war unthinkable.

Far better, he insists, to complete its construction and let the world know of its existence than to hide it.

Especially with the recent talk of a United Nations being established after the war's end, the bomb could be a powerful deterrent against future wars.

It could be a force for good.

Perhaps he's still in the grip of the "technically sweet problem", or perhaps he genuinely believes in the bomb's ability to end all wars.

Either way, Oppenheimer's argument wins out, as it always does.

Finally, in July of 1945, work on "the gadget" is completed.

All that remains is a test.

Alamogordo, New Mexico, was chosen as the site.

Formerly Apache country, it's known by the handful of locals by its spanish name - El Jornado del Muerto.

"The Journey of Death."

Oppenheimer names the site "Trinity".

The test is set for 4 am, July 16th.

In the weeks leading up to it, a 100 foot tower is constructed to house the bomb.

Bunkers are built for cameras to to record the blast.

The night of the test, however, a fierce electrical storm breaks out over the state.

The technicians and Army officials worry that lightning might set off an accidental detonation.

As they wait out the storm, the scientists amuse themselves by wagering on the results.

It costs 1 dollar to enter the pool. Edward Teller bets on a blast yield equal to 45,000 tons of TNT.

Oppenheimer bets lower, at 3,000 tons.

Enrico Fermi takes side bets on whether or not the state of New Mexico will be accidentally incinerated.

Finally, in the early morning, the countdown resumes and the scientists don their protective lenses.

Five.

Four.

Three.

Two.

One.

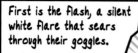

First is the flash, a silent white flare that sears through their goggles.

It's bright enough for a blind girl to see it, miles away on a distant road.

Next is the blast itself, which shakes the earth and reverberates like endless thunder over the hills.

The heat flash follows, burning the hair off the hands of scientists in the bunkers, 5 miles away.

A local rancher looking out his window wonders why the sun is rising in the wrong direction.

Finally, the great cloud rises up into the air, dwarfing the landscape and making even the mountains look small by comparison.

To the observers, it seems to take an eternity.

And everyone who sees it is forever changed by the experience.

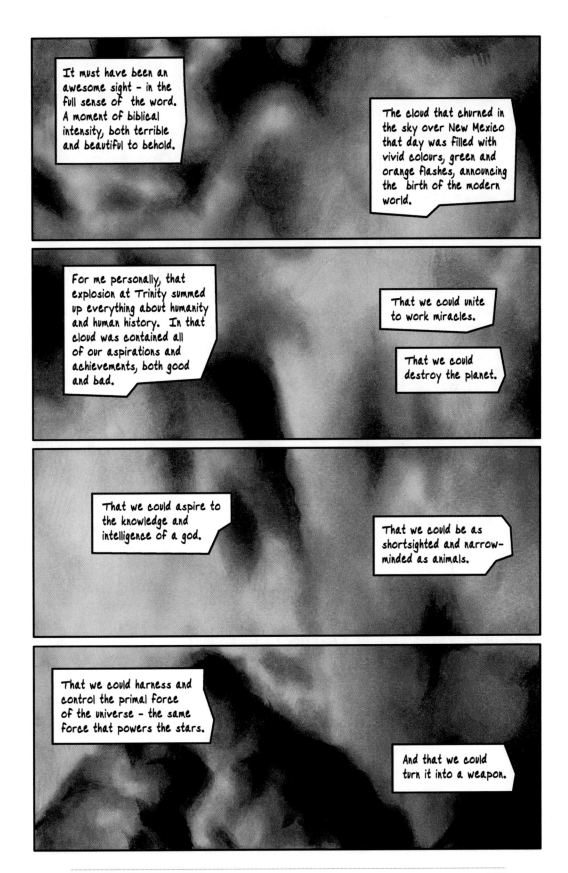

Oppenheimer later spoke about the reaction of the scientists as they witnessed that cloud:

"We knew the world would not be the same.

"A few people laughed. A few people cried.

"Most people were silent.

"I remembered the line from the Hindu scripture, the Bhagavad-Gita. Vishnu is trying to persuade the prince that he should do his duty and, to impress him, takes on his multi-armed form and says:

'Now I am become death, the destroyer of worlds.'

"I suppose we all thought that, one way or another."

He said that years later, near the end of his life.

It's a famous quote, but I don't know if I entirely believe him.

Oppenheimer was capable of playing many roles, including that of martyr.

Others who were there that day say that his reaction was one of pride at his accomplishment.

What I do know is that the events that followed were complicated.

But the bomb did that - made things complicated.

Within a month, the bomb was dropped on Hiroshima and Nagasaki, killing over 220,000 civilians and condemning thousands more to a lifetime of suffering.

But it ended the war.

The alternative, a land invasion of Japan, would have cost 500,000 lives.

Regardless of the ethics, the years immediately after World War II were good to Oppenheimer.

He was hailed as a national hero and reached the peak of his profession.

Appointed director of the Princeton Institute for Advanced Study, he even became Einstein's boss.

Now a man of great influence in scientific, military and political circles, he set about advising Washington on arms control, with the hope of finally using his creation as the force for good he intended it to be.

But then in 1949, the Soviet Union shocked the world with its own atomic test and helped usher in the start of the Cold War. Suddenly, arms control became the furthest thing from the minds of anyone in government.

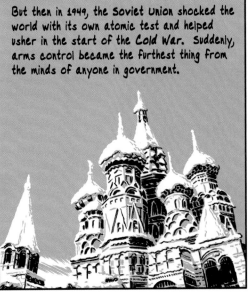

The 1950s brought America into the paranoia of the McCarthy era, and soon anyone with liberal sentiments was suspected of "working for the reds".

Eisenhower Urges Anti-Red Crusade

Expose Poisonous Propaganda, President's Plea to Publishers.

Rosenbergs, Doomed, To Appeal Jury Verdict

First U. S. Traitors Ever Sentenced to Death by Civil Court; Judge Denounces Deed.

Red Foes Face Abuse Always, Hoover Says

FBI Head Tells DAR Of 'Vile Attacks' on Those Speaking Out

Red Channels

The Report of COMMUNIST INFLUENCE ON RADIO AND TV

FBI J. ROBERT OPPENHEIMER SURVEILLANCE FILE

Oppenheimer wasn't exempt from the witch hunt.

His communist sympathies were a matter of F.B.I. record, and it wasn't long before he was brought before the *House Un-American Activities Committee.*

Despite testimonials from military and scientific officials, he was seen as a possible threat.

All his security clearances were revoked.

Now he would no longer have any say on arms control. Now no one in Washington would have anything to do with him.

All his power and influence were gone.

And he would never work on nuclear projects again.

In many ways, that loss of influence must have broken his spirit. He was, after all, a man used to being listened to.

A man whose whole life had been evidence of a rare and special destiny.

Now, as the U.S. continued development on newer and more destructive weapons like the hydrogen bomb, he had become irrelevant.

Haunted by his past, Oppenheimer aged quickly and died in 1967 of throat cancer.

Since that first test in 1945, there have been over 2050 nuclear detonations.

Some were conducted at sea, others deep underground.

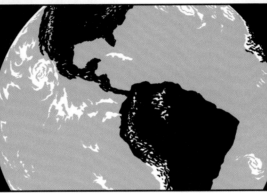

The largest of them carried more than 4000 times the destructive power of the bomb dropped on Hiroshima.

As a result of the fallout from all those tests, everyone on earth now carries trace elements of radioactivity - of strontium and tritium in our bodies.

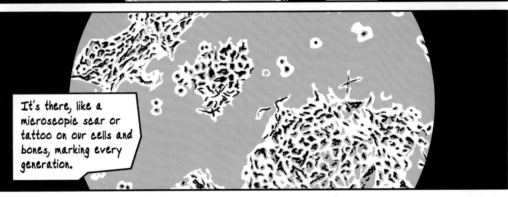

It's there, like a microscopic scar or tattoo on our cells and bones, marking every generation.

A tiny reminder of the efforts of 6000 men and women...

...of a fierce and terrible cloud that rose up into the morning air...

...and all the unanswerable questions that rose up with it, on that fateful day at Trinity.

TRINITY SITE
WHERE
THE WORLD'S FIRST
NUCLEAR DEVICE
WAS EXPLODED ON
JULY 16, 1945

Analyze

(1) One of the challenges writers face is how to effectively represent the passage of time. On the second page of "Trinity," Cho's first three panels depict December 1938, August 1939, and December 1941, respectively. How does he keep these big shifts in time from being jarring or disrupting the narrative? What visual techniques does he use to help manage this?

(2) At the bottom of the third page, we see three consecutive shots of Oppenheimer's face, each one a little more of a close-up. What effect—what meaning—is Cho trying to achieve by this sequence?

(3) It's certainly fitting that the test site for "the gadget" is Alamogordo, New Mexico, a place locals call *El Jornada del Muerto*, or "The Journey of Death." But Oppenheimer calls this site "Trinity." What connections/meanings do you attach to that word, and why might Trinity be an equally appropriate site for the first atomic bomb explosion?

(4) So much of this excerpt is done in gray tones, but then Cho includes a full page of red-hued panels. Why did he withhold color until that point? Does the way the text appears on that particular page relate to the color choice? How so?

Explore

(1) The entire fourteen-page story of *Trinity* was selected by Neil Gaiman to appear in *The Best American Comics 2010*. Cho was also asked to provide the cover art for that book. Find a copy of the cover at Amazon.com or elsewhere online. How do you see his *Trinity* story informing this cover illustration? What elements of this teen angst image link up with the Manhattan Project and Oppenheimer's story? If you had to guess at what type of statement or commentary Cho is making with the cover image, what is it? Why?

(2) In light of the historical facts this story reveals, would you have made the same choice Oppenheimer did, to go ahead with finishing the bomb despite it being clear that no one else on the planet would have one for years, if ever? What about the idea of dropping an atomic bomb on Nagasaki and Hiroshima to save American troops who would be lost through a land invasion of Japan? What factors do you need to consider before making a decision like this? Could you make such a decision?

(3) In an August 2014 interview with Multiversity Comics, Cho talks about his new graphic novel *Shoplifter*: "I've always liked two-tone work because it allows me to focus on things like mood and atmosphere. I'm better at depicting interior states or subtleties of mood in two-tone than I am with a full colour palette, so it was a perfect fit with this story which is focused on one

character and is fairly quiet in tone. I often think I can draw a more expressive range of emotions with just two colours than I can trying to juggle harmonies in full colour. I don't find it limiting in any way but rather the opposite." How do you see this same idea playing out in "Trinity?"

DERF

My Friend Dahmer

Derf is the pen name for the comic artist John Backderf. Born in 1959, Backderf grew up in Richfield, Ohio, and later attended the Art Institute of Pittsburgh and Ohio State University. As an artist, his images have appeared on T-shirts and CD covers, and in periodicals ranging from the *Wall Street Journal* to *Guitar Player*. He is best known for his weekly strip *The City*, which appeared in over 100 alt-weekly newspapers from 1990 to 2014. In addition to *The City*, he has published graphic novels, including *My Friend Dahmer*, excerpted here, which recounts the author's childhood experience with Jeffrey Dahmer, a boy who would later become a serial killer and cannibal. Backderf presently lives in Cleveland, Ohio.

I FIRST MET **JEFF DAHMER** IN THE **SEVENTH GRADE**, WHEN THE KIDS FROM THE DISTRICT'S THREE ELEMENTARY SCHOOLS WERE **STIRRED TOGETHER** IN THE HORMONAL SOUP THAT WAS **JUNIOR HIGH**.

EASTVIEW JUNIOR HIGH
WELCOME BACK STUDENTS

HE WAS A **NOBODY**. ONE OF THOSE **SHY KIDS** WHO TURNED INTO **SOCIAL INVALIDS** WHEN THAT FIRST BLAST OF ADOLESCENCE HIT, MEEKLY ACCEPTED THEIR FATE, AND BECAME INVISIBLE. IT WAS **MONTHS** INTO THE SCHOOL YEAR BEFORE I NOTICED HIM **AT ALL**.

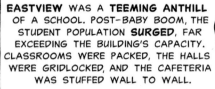

EASTVIEW WAS A **TEEMING ANTHILL** OF A SCHOOL. POST–BABY BOOM, THE STUDENT POPULATION **SURGED**, FAR EXCEEDING THE BUILDING'S CAPACITY. CLASSROOMS WERE PACKED, THE HALLS WERE GRIDLOCKED, AND THE CAFETERIA WAS STUFFED WALL TO WALL.

IT WAS QUITE A **SHOCK** TO THE SYSTEM, AFTER THE COMFORTABLE FAMILIARITY OF THE COZY ELEMENTARY SCHOOLS. IF YOU WERE **SHY** AND **SLOW** TO **MAKE FRIENDS**, YOU WERE VIRTUALLY **TRAMPLED** BY THE THRONG.

FOR **MOST** KIDS, IT WAS AN OPPORTUNITY TO MAKE **NEW FRIENDS** BY THE BUSHEL. **SEVERAL** OF THE GUYS I MET DURING THIS TIME WOULD BE **LIFELONG PALS**.

DAHMER **DIDN'T** MAKE NEW FRIENDS.

AS FAR AS I COULD TELL...

...HE DIDN'T HAVE ANY FRIENDS, **PERIOD**.

HE WAS THE **LONELIEST** KID I'D EVER MET.

REVER

HUFF! PUFF!

DAHMER LIVED IN RURAL **BATH, OHIO**, IN THE ROLLING COUNTRYSIDE JUST OUTSIDE GRIMY, CRUMBLING AKRON. THE RUBBER CITY WAS AN INDUSTRIAL POWERHOUSE GONE **BUST** IN THE GREAT **SEVENTIES RECESSION**.

TIMES WERE **TOUGH**.

THE TIRE FACTORIES WERE **CLOSING**. ONCE BUSTLING, DOWNTOWN AKRON WAS NOW A **GHOST TOWN** OF BOARDED-UP STORES. PEOPLE WERE **LEAVING** THE AREA IN DROVES. AKRON WAS **DYING**.

BUT OUT HERE IN THE COUNTRY **LIFE WAS GOOD**, ESPECIALLY FOR A **KID**. BEAUTIFUL, DEEP **WOODS** AND OPEN **FIELDS AND MEADOWS** THAT STRETCHED ON FOR MILES IN EVERY DIRECTION, AND **COZY NEIGHBORHOODS** WHERE EVERYONE KNEW YOUR NAME.

IT WAS THE **UNLIKELIEST** OF **BREEDING GROUNDS** FOR THE MOST DEPRAVED SERIAL KILLER SINCE **JACK THE RIPPER.**

CLICK

HOW DO YOU LIKE EASTVIEW, JEFF?

S'OKAY.

LIONEL WAS A CHEMIST, HARDWORKING AND DRIVEN. HE WAS A **NICE MAN**, BUT HAD A FORCEFUL PERSONALITY AND AN INTIMIDATING INTELLECT.

MY DAD WAS A CHEMIST, TOO, SO I KNOW WELL **THE TYPE**, MORE COMFORTABLE WITH **TEST TUBES** THAN WITH **TEENAGE SONS.** I NEVER SAW THAT MUCH OF LIONEL EITHER.

JOYCE WAS A HOUSEWIFE WHO WAS **CHAFING** IN THAT ROLE, LIKE **MANY** MOMS IN THE EARLY SEVENTIES.

SHE WAS ALWAYS PLEASANT TO ME, BUT SHE WAS **ODD.** VERY **MOODY** AND **FRAGILE.** IT WAS OBVIOUS SHE WAS LUGGING AROUND SOME **HEAVY BAGGAGE.**

BUT THERE WERE LOTS OF **DAMAGED MOMS** IN TOWN.

THE DAHMER HOUSE WAS **SHOEHORNED** ONTO A STEEP TWO-ACRE **HILLSIDE** COVERED IN **THICK WOODS.**

AT THE BOTTOM OF THE HILL WAS A LARGE **SUBURBAN NEIGHBORHOOD**, STRAIGHT OUT OF "THE BRADY BRUNCH."

TIDY RANCH HOMES, CLOSELY PACKED TOGETHER. WELL-KEPT LAWNS AND **LOTS** OF KIDS.

BUT DAHMER'S HOUSE FACED A **STEEP COUNTRY ROAD** THAT WASN'T SAFE FOR KIDS TO BIKE OR EVEN WALK ALONG.

ALL THAT COULD BE SEEN OF IT FROM THE ROAD WAS THE **BLANK FACADE** OF THE GARAGE. IT WAS AS IF THE HOUSE ITSELF **MIRRORED** JEFF'S **ISOLATION**.

AND **INSIDE** THE HOUSE...

...ALL WAS **NOT** WELL.

WHO CAN TURN THE WORLD ON WITH HER SMILE ♪ ♫

JOYCE, I AM **NOT** GOING TO HAVE THIS ARGUMENT... **AGAIN!**

SEVENTH GRADE, EIGHTH GRADE, NINTH GRADE — **ALL** THROUGH JUNIOR HIGH, DAHMER **DIDN'T** STAND OUT IN **ANY** WAY. HE WAS JUST PART OF THE ADOLESCENT MASS, A PIECE OF THE SCENERY. HE SELDOM TALKED. HE DID HIS WORK, PLAYED TRUMPET IN THE BAND, WAS A MEMBER OF THE TENNIS TEAM... HE **BARELY** MADE A **RIPPLE**.

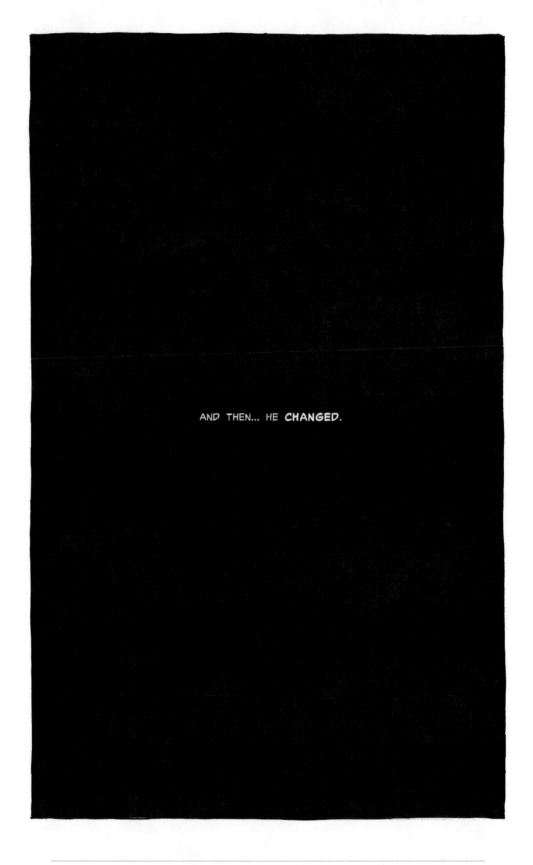

Analyze

(1) How surprised where you when Dahmer took the fetal pig out of his backpack at home? Why do you suspect he took the dead pig?

(2) This excerpt prominently showcases bullying in schools. How did bullying affect Dahmer? How did bullying affect the author? How do the visuals reveal the impact of that bullying?

(3) Considering how much emphasis the author puts on social isolation and family dysfunction, is it fair to say that Dahmer is presented as a tragic figure, a person who was deeply and irrevocably damaged as a child?

(4) In an interview, Backderf says, "I don't think we do ourselves any favors by writing people like Dahmer off as monsters, because that implies that it was inevitable that he became one." What does Backderf mean? Why is this an important distinction?

Explore

(1) Even though Backderf knew Dahmer in his youth, he still conducted primary research to write this graphic novel. In the author's notes, he lists sources used. Locate a primary source or two that details the facts of Dahmer's later life (such as a magazine exposé, a book chapter, or newspaper article). Does learning more about what Dahmer did change your understanding of Dahmer in the comic?

(2) Revisit the panel that shows the science classroom where Dahmer and Backderf are sitting together. Now visit Backderf's website, www.derfcity.com, and look at the picture on the "About" page. Which of the two comic characters does the author more resemble? Assume for a moment that Derf purposefully depicted himself in a way that resembles Dahmer. What might that artistic choice mean?

(3) This comic is called *My Friend Dahmer*, yet Backderf and Dahmer don't appear to be friends in any traditional sense. Why does the author use the word "friend" to describe their relationship? Is he using the term ironically? Does it indicate a personal definition of friendship, something outside of its traditional definition?

(4) In a time when Facebook helps us acquire "friends" we've never met, the term itself has become imprecise. Write a short essay that explains what a friend is. What is required, in your opinion, for two people to be considered "friends"?

Politics

Today, the idea of a person being "political" often means that one is engaged in and informed about national politics. A person may be "political" if they have a large investment in a particular candidate. A person may also be "political" if they voice opinions about national policies. Its verbal form—"politicize"—often suggests an attitude of manipulation. For example, an environmental group may "politicize" photographs of young polar bears stranded on an ice floe to influence how the public views global warming. But the term *politics*, when used in an academic setting, encompasses power of all kinds.

In the terms of this textbook, politics is certainly about governance, but also about influence. Yet it's also about the power distribution within communities as well as the complex interrelationships between people: how power is shared—or not shared—among the rich and poor, black and white, conservatives and liberals.

One of the greatest appeals of literature is narrative. Everyone loves a good story. But a sensitive reading of a good story—be it a traditional text or a graphic narrative—often reveals political relationships essential to the world represented in the story. For many students, the exploration of political relationships in stories prepares them to examine political relationships in the world they inhabit. Literature, then, becomes a means to understand power structures in society.

Consider for a moment how influential novels like *Uncle Tom's Cabin* or *Brave New World* ignited debates and influenced culture. Likewise, Margaret Atwood's landmark novel *The Handmaid's Tale* asked a generation to reconsider the role of personal responsibility regarding women's rights and how the individual plays a role in a repressive society.

As with traditional literature, great graphic narratives ask readers to examine present-day culture through the political structures represented in their stories. Kim Deitch's controversial "Ready to Die" examines the debate about the death penalty, a polarizing political issue that concerns race, poverty, and divergent concepts of justice. "In the Shadow of No Towers," Art Spiegelman's reflection on 9/11, raises questions about military power, propaganda campaigns, and government responsibility. Peter Bagge's "The War on Fornication" explores concepts of personal freedom and oppression, particularly as they apply to gender issues.

Social power and alienation. Wealth and poverty. Privilege and oppression. The graphic selections in this section cover these important issues—particularly how political forces shape the world of these narratives. Who has power? And who doesn't? How does power shape a society's values and arrange its communities? One thing seems certain—there are no easy answers to any of these questions.

KIM DEITCH

"Ready to Die"

The son of a UPA animator,* Kim Deitch is a god-father of the underground comix movement. In 1967, Deitch found an audience writing and drawing for the *East Village Other* with work that has been described in *The New York Times* as "crazy, invigorating stuff." His early work includes strips that represent the psychedelic trends of the 1960s: Waldo the Cat and Uncle Ed, and the India Rubber Man, for example. In 2003, he received an Eisner Award. His graphic novel *The Boulevard of Broken Dreams*—a satirical history of early American animation studios—was named by *Time* magazine as one of the 100 best English-language graphic novels ever written.

---

*United Productions of America, an animation studio active from the 1940s through the 1970s, had less of an impact than that of Disney and Warner Bros.

READY TO DIE

BY Kim Deitch

COLORING: RHEA PATTON.

Kim Deitch.

Lethal Injection DIE

THERE'S NOT A WHOLE LOT IN JARRATT, OTHER THAN THE GREENSVILLE CORRECTIONAL CENTER, WHERE EXECUTIONS ARE CARRIED OUT IN THE STATE OF VIRGINIA.

I WAS THERE TO WITNESS THE LAST ACT IN A TRAGEDY THAT BEGAN IN ANOTHER SMALL VIRGINIA TOWN.

CHATHAM, VA: ON JANUARY 29, 1993, RONALD FITZGERALD SNAPPED. A JEALOUS RAMPAGE OVER HIS GIRLFRIEND TRIGGERED SIX HOURS OF MURDER, ROBBERY, AND RAPE. ALL HIS VICTIMS HAD ONE WAY OR ANOTHER FUELED HIS JEALOUSY. IT WAS THE WORST CRIME SPREE IN CHATHAM'S HISTORY.

HE BEGAN LOOKING, WITHOUT SUCCESS, FOR A MAN WHO, HE SAID, HAD TAUNTED HIM, SAYING "YOU'RE FEEDING MY BABY" AND "I'VE HAD YOUR WOMAN."

AT 6 A.M. HE KILLED A MAN NAMED COY WHITE, WHILE A 13-YEAR-OLD GIRL WATCHED.

HE THEN DROVE THE GIRL TO A SECLUDED AREA, RAPED HER AND LEFT HER LOCKED IN A CAR TRUNK.

NEXT HE WALKED TO THE MAIN ROAD AND FLAGGED DOWN HUIE MORRISON'S TAXI.

MORRISON'S BODY WAS LATER FOUND IN A CREEK, SHOT THREE TIMES.

FITZGERALD THEN DROVE THE CAB TO THE HOME OF THE GIRLFRIEND OF THE MAN HE WAS STILL LOOKING FOR.

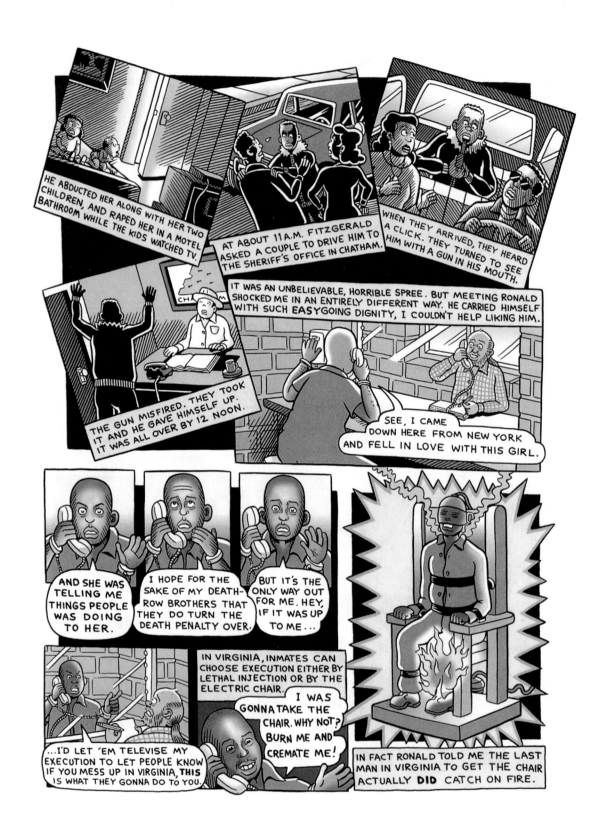

Politics

I'D FOUND OUT PLENTY. AND YET I WAS STILL HAUNTED BY CERTAIN THINGS RONALD TOLD ME.

YOU KNOW, I'VE GROWN A LOT IN THE LAST FOUR YEARS.

I'M NOT THE SAME PERSON.

I'VE MADE A LOT OF FRIENDS ON DEATH ROW, AND I'M GONNA MISS MY DEATH-ROW SOLDIERS.

SO I DECIDED TO VISIT SUSSEX 1, A MAXIMUM SECURITY UNIT NOT FAR FROM THE PRISON WHERE RONALD WAS EXECUTED.

SUSSEX 1 IS ACTUALLY A CLUSTER OF SMALL, IDENTICAL PRISON UNITS CALLED PODS. ONE OF THESE PODS, A CHILLING PLACE OF STAINLESS STEEL AND ANTISEPTIC ODORS, IS VIRGINIA'S DEATH ROW.

DEREK BARNABEI, #227108, HAD THIS TO SAY ABOUT THE DEATH PENALTY IN VIRGINIA:

IS IT A RACIAL THING? YES! IS IT A MONETARY THING? YES! THEY ARE EXECUTING THE WEAKEST PEOPLE IN OUR SOCIETY.

DEREK TOLD ME THAT RONALD ONCE SAVED HIS LIFE BY TAKING A "SHANK" FOR HIM.

AND HE TOLD ME ABOUT VIRGINIA'S NOTORIOUS 21-DAY RULE.

IT MEANS YOU CAN'T INTRODUCE ANY NEW EVIDENCE MORE THAN 21 DAYS AFTER TRIAL. EXCEPT AS A CLEMENCY REQUEST AT THE VERY END.

STEVE ROACH, #225822, DID MOST OF RONALD'S TATTOOING.

JUST BEING SENTENCED TO DEATH IS ENOUGH TO MAKE ANYONE LOSE THEIR RIGHT STATE OF MIND. BUT FORTUNATELY I'VE HAD THE RIGHT KIND OF FRIENDS WHO UNDERSTAND WHAT WE'RE ALL GOING THROUGH. LOSING FITZGERALD PUT A DENT IN THAT. HE WAS A FUNNY GUY, AND YOU NEED THAT HERE.

See you at the Crossroads

R.I.P

TOMMY STRICKLER, #178579, HAS ALREADY BEEN TRANSFERRED TO GREENSVILLE FOR EXECUTION ON TWO SEPARATE OCCASIONS.

WHEN YOU GET DOWN TO GREENSVILLE, THEY ACT LIKE THEY'RE GETTING READY TO HAVE A PARTY.

AND THEN WHEN YOU GET A STAY, THEY'RE WALKIN' AROUND WITH THEIR HEADS DOWN LIKE THEY'RE VERY UNHAPPY THAT THEIR PARTY GOT MESSED UP.

ABOUT FITZGERALD, HIS FORMER NEIGHBOR ON THE ROW, HE SAID, "ABOUT TWO DAYS AFTER HE WAS EXECUTED, I WAS WATCHIN' TV; AND I CALLED HIM TO TURN THE CHANNEL."

HEY FITZGERALD!

"AND THEN IT DAWNED ON ME THAT HE WASN'T THERE ANYMORE."

BUT THE THING THAT STAYS WITH ME, AFTER COVERING THIS STORY, IS THE WARM FEELING I ENDED UP HAVING FOR RONALD'S FAMILY. I VISITED HIS MOTHER AND AUNTS TWO WEEKS AFTER THE EXECUTION.

WHILE WE TALKED, THEY SHOWED ME PHOTOS OF RONALD TAKEN WITH HIS MOTHER AND SISTER ON THE DAY HE DIED.

RONNIE'S A KID WE'RE ALL DEFINITELY GONNA MISS.

Nancy Fitzgerald

THE SAD PART ABOUT OUR FAMILY IS, WE'RE MISSING ALL THE MALES.

Dorothy Coles Noel

JUST THE OTHER DAY YOU SAW HIM AS A KID AND NOW HE'S LAYIN' IN A COFFIN.

Lois Ann Coles

WHAT MAKES ME SAD IS THAT HE WAS UP AT 6:30 THAT DAY. HE WAS SO EXCITED THAT HIS FAMILY WAS COMING TO SEE HIM.

...WE'RE SORRY FOR THE VICTIMS, BUT WE LOVED HIM TO THE END."

Jackie Coles

AND WE STILL LOVE HIM.

His mother, Mae Fitzgerald

Analyze

(1) Based on the comic's illustrations (such as the expression of disbelief and horror on Deitch's face in the first panel) and the text (such as the use of the word "tragedy" to describe Ronald Fitzgerald's situation, also in the first panel), define Deitch's position on the death penalty.

(2) Deitch calls the execution of Ronald Fitzgerald "the last act in a tragedy." In what sense is this a tragedy? Consider that the comic situates Fitzgerald's execution as the punishment for his "jealous rampage" in which he murdered two men and raped a woman and a thirteen-year-old girl.

(3) One of the central controversies of this graphic reportage concerns the presentation of Ronald Fitzgerald as a man with "such easygoing dignity" that Deitch "couldn't help liking him." How do you, as a reader, reconcile the images of Fitzgerald's murderous rampage with the presentation of him as a sympathetic, family-oriented man in prison?

(4) Though "Ready to Die" is presented as first-person reporting, it is also an argument in which the author presents the humanity of men condemned to die. Did this piece of graphic reportage change your ideas about capital punishment? If so, which panels were most influential?

Explore

(1) As a general rule of thumb, the largest panels in a comic are devoted to the most important moments. Review the largest panels in this comic, which occupy one-third to one-half of a page. In your opinion, why are the events in these panels given the most space? Conversely, why are Fitzgerald's crimes given so little space, with ten small, overlapping images?

(2) In this comic, whom does the death penalty help? One victim's relative says, "The law was carried out. It's nothing to celebrate." Consider the perspectives of Fitzgerald's family, the victims and their families, and the men incarcerated with Fitzgerald.

(3) In your opinion, do the tools of the graphic reporter (a writer who uses both text *and* illustration) allow the reporting to be more subjective or more objective? That is, does illustration tend to accentuate the personal bias of the author or limit it by tying illustrations to actual events?

(4) The comic artist Harvey Pekar once speculated that first-person accounts in graphic narratives might have unique power: "I started theorizing about comic books and what else could be done with them. . . . I started thinking about doing stories that were realistic, and the best realistic stories I could do were autobiographical. It seemed that the more accurately I wrote about my life the better the story came out." In your opinion is Deitch's first-person account of witnessing Fitzgerald's execution and its effects more powerful than a journalistic depiction of the events by themselves, without Deitch including himself as a figure in the comic? Support your answer with examples.

NEUFELD

JOSH NEUFELD

A.D.: New Orleans After the Deluge

Josh Neufeld is a Brooklyn-based alternative cartoonist most famous for his illustrations of nonfiction works in which he tackles such topics as Hurricane Katrina, the media, the world of high finance, and international travel. The best-selling graphic nonfiction book *The Influencing Machine: Brooke Gladstone on the Media* is one of the many books he's illustrated. He's also the first "comics journalist" to receive a Knight-Wallace Fellowship at the University of Michigan. As a cultural ambassador in the U.S. Department of State's Speaker and Specialist Program, he's run workshops in Burma, Algeria, Bahrain, Egypt, and Israel.

436

Politics

Politics

Analyze

(1) Color is a key element in this story. In fact, Neufeld told *The New York Times*, "I tried to use the colors to help the readers through, to create mood." The section in this book primarily has a mellow green cast to it. What might Neufeld intend with that choice, in contrast to the last image in the book—a FEMA (Federal Emergency Management Agency) trailer covered with Mardi Gras beads, a fleur-de-lis, and a Mardi Gras flag in traditional purple, gold, and green? How might these scenes work differently if they were in straight black and white?

(2) Why do Abbas and Darnell stay behind despite being told to flee? Do their actions seem to represent the norm for this situation? How do you suspect their friendship is going to be tested? What do you think is going to happen next?

(3) Why does the author include full-page panels showing a single image (also known as a "splash page")? What is the effect of this illustration choice? How does layout—the decision to render some panels large, other panels small—contribute to the meaning of the story? What do you make of that final image in this excerpt that only has the word "G'night"?

(4) If you had to select a different section in this textbook for this story to appear, which would you choose? Why? If you had to lead a discussion on this story for a group of eager, smart middle schoolers, what topics would you most focus on?

Explore

(1) In *A.D.*, Neufeld presents an argument about the effectiveness of the government's response to Hurricane Katrina. What is the position of Neufeld's argument? How are its claims rendered and supported in illustration? Because illustration is highly subjective—more so than photography—do you find Neufeld's argument compelling?

(2) Use the Internet to view photographs or videos of Hurricane Katrina, and then revisit the excerpt from *A.D.* that shows its devastation. What differences do you find in each way of witnessing? What similarities? Which do you find more effective?

(3) Speak with people who have experienced a large-scale disaster such as a tornado, earthquake, fire, flood, and so on. Find out firsthand what choices they made—good, bad, or otherwise. How did they feel about the experience? What did they learn? Feel free to take notes and share what you discovered with others.

(4) *A.D.* originally appeared as a serialized web comic in *Smith Magazine*. Visit http://www.smithmag.net/afterthedeluge/ to see the original artwork and discover more about the *A.D.* story. How does having such access to the author as well as the "story behind the story" affect your experience with the text? Take a moment to watch the "How *A.D.* Got Made" video. Does your understanding of the comic change when you see how Neufeld captured the lives of real people in his book? Would the story feel as powerful if Neufeld had created entirely fictional characters? Why or why not?

PETER KUPER

"Ceci N'est Pas une Comic"

Peter Kuper is a political cartoonist and illustrator who often draws inspiration from personal observations and experience. He has created many graphic novels, including *Diario de Oaxaca*, which chronicles a teachers' strike in Mexico, and *Drawn to New York*, an illustrated history of New York from the late 1970s to the 2000s. He has adapted the stories of Franz Kafka into graphic form. His paintings are regularly featured on the cover of *The New Yorker* magazine. But he is perhaps best known as a regular contributor to *Mad* magazine, where he draws the "Spy vs. Spy" comic.

Ceci n'est pas un comic

A G.W.BUSH ADMINISTRATION RETROSPECTIVE *

Analyze

(1) The comic "Ceci n'est pas une Comic" by Peter Kuper draws its title from a painting produced by the Belgian artist René Magritte, which is included in the first panel. In Magritte's original painting, an image of a pipe appears above the slogan "Ceci n'est pas une pipe," which translates to "This is not a pipe." When asked the meaning of the slogan, Magritte explained that the pipe—though realistic—was only the "representation" of a pipe and not the pipe itself. "Ceci n'est pas une comic" means, roughly, "This is not a comic." In what sense is Kuper's work not a comic?

(2) Magritte's original painting presents a realistic representation of a pipe. What is the relationship between each poster image and its accompanying text in the rest of the comic? Are some pairings representational—in which the text accurately describes the image? Are some pairings ironic—in which the textual meaning is roughly the opposite of the meaning suggested by the image? Are some lines of text sardonic overstatements? Which is the most disturbing combination of image and text?

(3) The comic is a critique of the Bush presidency from 2000 to 2008 in which the author argues that the administration misled the American public and mishandled its power. The argument is presented, primarily, with iconic images paired with slogans. Aside from the slogans and an "exit" sign, the comic contains no text. Do you find this comic argument, with its minimal text, as persuasive as a traditional written argument? If so, how do these images communicate meaning as effectively as an argument more firmly based in language?

(4) The comic includes multiple panels in which the gallery visitors—the man and woman—are observed by a red video camera. Why include this camera so prominently?

Explore

(1) The comic incorporates different graphic styles to create the posters: some posters include photographic elements (such as the explosion), some are pure icon (such as the peace symbol), some are cartoon representations (such as the polar bear clutching an iceberg), and some are flat comic drawings (such as the homeless man). In your opinion, which graphic style carries the most power? Why?

(2) The comic is set inside of an art gallery, suggesting that one role of contemporary art is to critique government power structures. Create a list of other places or venues where writers, artists, speakers, and individuals can effectively critique government power.

(3) The graphic posters in the comic, largely, critique the official government narrative of Bush-era news events. Respond to the comic with three posters

of your own. Your three posters can critique a political group, a government stance, a corporate ad campaign, the opinions of celebrities, or another powerful narrative that originates from a source of cultural power. Consider how your three posters together can create an effective argument that asks readers to reconsider the message of a political group, a government organization, a corporation, and so on.

ART SPIEGELMAN

"In the Shadow of No Towers"

Born in Sweden in 1948, Art Spiegelman is a New York–based cartoonist best known for his 1992 Pulitzer Prize–winning graphic novel *Maus*, which creatively depicts his father's experience as a Holocaust survivor. The critical attention this award brought to the marginalized comics industry quickly made Spiegelman one of the strongest comics advocates in the world. He furthered his reputation by introducing many new cartoonists by coediting eleven issues of *Raw* and serving as an editor and teacher at the School of the Visual Arts in New York City. His popular lecture "What the %@&*! Happened to Comics?" has influenced scholars and serves as a guided tour to the evolution of the field. Spiegelman argues that comics truly matter and that they are becoming more important: "Comics echo the way the brain works. People think in iconographic images, not in holograms, and people think in bursts of language, not in paragraphs." Some initial readers were troubled by "In the Shadow of No Towers," his response to the 9/11 attacks in Manhattan, though many admire the clarity of his wit, the evocativeness of his images, and the accuracy of his commentary regarding this national tragedy.

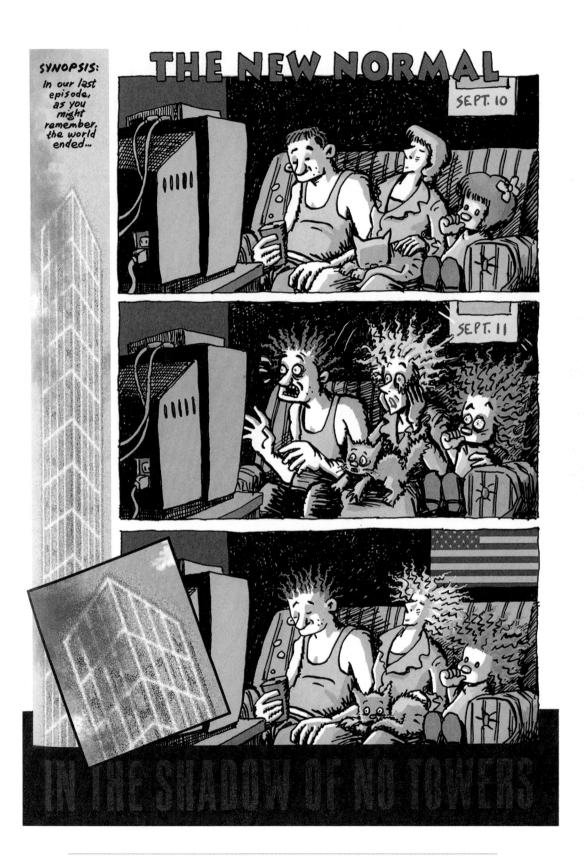

I still see the glowing tower, awesome as it collapses—

I was sure we were gonna die...

I've always sorta suspected it, but that morning really convinced me...

My wife, my daughter and I are rushing from the bomb site. We hear a roar, like a waterfall, and look back. The air smells of death—

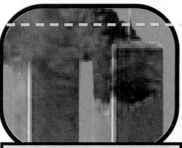

Those crumbling towers burned their way into everyone's brain. but I live on the outskirts of Ground Zero and first saw it all live—unmediated.

Maybe it's just a question of scale. Even on a large tv, the towers aren't much bigger than, say, Dan Rather's head...

Logos, on the other hand, look enormous on tv; it's a medium almost as well-suited as comics for dealing in abstractions.

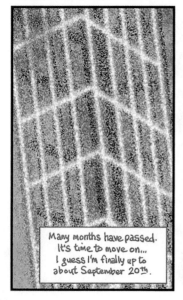

Many months have passed. It's time to move on... I guess I'm finally up to about September 20th.

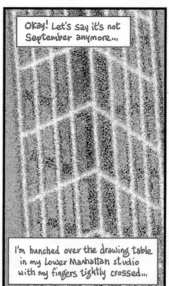

Okay! Let's say it's not September anymore...

I'm hunched over the drawing table in my Lower Manhattan studio with my fingers tightly crossed...

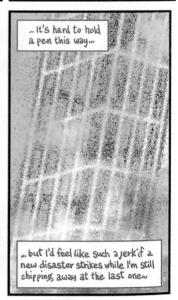

...It's hard to hold a pen this way...

... but I'd feel like such a jerk if a new disaster strikes while I'm still chipping away at the last one...

IN THE SHADOW OF NO TOWERS

EQUALLY TERRORIZED BY AL-QAEDA AND BY HIS OWN GOVERNMENT...

Our Hero looks over some ancient comics pages instead of working. He dozes off and relives his ringside seat to that day's disaster yet again, trying to figure out what he actually saw...

Analyze

(1) Early on, the author mentions that the 9/11 tragedy they witnessed was "unmediated." What does the author mean by that claim? Why is it important to point out? How much news do you consume that is unmediated?

(2) In its first three panels, the comic presents an American family whose sense of reality and well-being is impacted by televised images. What changes are evident in the family, as they sit on the couch, between the first and the third images? How have the events of 9/11 affected them?

(3) The author explains how, many months later, he sits at his drawing table in lower Manhattan with his "fingers tightly crossed," noting too that it's "hard to hold a pen this way." What comment is the author making about the relationship between art and tragedy? Is it important that "many months passed" versus this being an immediate artistic response to 9/11?

(4) Unlike many of the comics included in this textbook, the author consciously uses a variety of presentation styles—realism, caricature, political, abstraction, graphic advertisement, and so on—to convey the experience of 9/11. Why do you think the author chose so many styles? How do the various styles help frame, define, or enhance the story's meaning?

Explore

(1) Why is 9/11 such an important topic in American history? Spend a few moments to research some of the facts about the event. Consider video clips, interviews, news articles, and personal accounts as good possibilities for your source material. Reflecting on what you discovered and its relationship to this text, how did 9/11 affect Americans? The rest of the world? This comic's creator? Your own family? Yourself?

(2) In the "Jihad Brand Footwear" advertisement, the author suggests that American anxiety about 9/11 has been intentionally heightened by media images. Much in the same way that ads create a sense of desire or anticipation in the viewer, over-coverage of news events can create a sense of fear or impending dread for the audience. In your opinion, do you believe the twenty-four-hour news cycle—with constant updates on TV, the Internet, and smartphone apps—is more beneficial (in keeping the public informed) or detrimental (in creating unnecessary fear or in treating news stories like a type of entertainment)?

(3) Televised images replayed in constant rotation can create something like an artificial shared memory. While sitting at his desk, the author of this strip tries "to figure out what he actually saw," as opposed to what he watched on TV. Most people entering college today are too young to have any firsthand memories of the national 9/11 experience. For your generation, what televised or Internet events are so pervasive and compelling that you—and others— feel as though you somehow participated in them?

PETER BAGGE

"The War on Fornication"

Best known for his darkly humorous, satirical style and exaggerated artwork, Peter Bagge is an American cartoonist born in 1957. His initial notoriety came from being heralded as a Seattle-based alternative comics legend in the 1990s thanks to his examination of the Gen-X world through his series *Hate*, which stars slacker Buddy Bradley. His libertarian leanings inspired him to enter the political arena with the graphic biography *Woman Rebel: The Margaret Sanger Story*, which offers a profile of the social maverick who founded the first birth control clinic in 1916. "The War on Fornication," included here, expands on Bagge's exploration of this controversial subject. He continues his ongoing commentary on the American political landscape in *Everybody Is Stupid Except for Me and Other Acute Observations*.

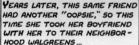

If public humiliation is the goal, why not go all out and give female customers the full Taliban treatment?

Oh, wait -- we wage wars against societies that harbor such primitive views on sexuality. I forgot!

Plan B has revived a war against contraceptives in general -- due in part to false comparisons with RU-486, which _is_ an "abortion pill"!

Rather than racing for a waiting egg, sperm are more likely the ones who have to wait -- sometimes up to five days -- before an egg is released from the ovaries...

Plan B is basically a "hot shot" of the same hormones used in birth control pills, which prevents the egg from being released, thus preventing fertilization.

If fertilization does occur, however, Plan B is likely to prevent the zygote from implanting itself on the uterine wall, where it would then evolve into an embryo, and then a fetus...

...And not everyone agrees as to whether a fertilized egg counts as the beginning of a life, since it isn't viable until implantation. But if a zygote is a "baby," does preventing implantation count as an abortion?

I'm personally not going to lose any sleep over this hypothetical technicality, but there are some folks who do...

...All of whom are anti-abortion activists, whose recent bestowal of full-blown personhood upon zygotes is their reason to oppose emergency contraceptives altogether.

This issue has also re-exposed the fact that many "pro-life" activists are opposed to the use of contraceptives in general...

THE CRAZIEST THING ABOUT ABORTION IS THAT WE'RE ALL OVER THE MAP WHEN IT COMES TO THAT DIFFICULT SUBJECT...

I'M **AGAINST** ABORTION... | EVEN THOUGH I HAD ONE **LAST WEEK**... BUT **LEMME TELL YA:** IT WAS **GROSS!** | TECHNICALLY I'M **PRO-CHOICE**... | THOUGH I'D **KILL** ANY WOMAN WHO KILLED **MY BABY**... **MY D.N.A.** IS **SACRED** TO ME! | I THINK IT'S **MURDER**... | NOT THAT A WOMAN SHOULD GO TO **JAIL** FOR HAVING ONE, OF COURSE... **THAT WOULD BE MEAN!** | I SAY ALL **ILLEGAL ALIENS** SHOULD BE **ABORTED!** | DON'T YOU MEAN **"DEPORTED"?** **THAT TOO!**

WHAT THE DEBATE IS *REALLY* ALL ABOUT IS POLICING OTHER PEOPLE'S **SEXUAL BEHAVIOR** -- WHICH WOULD PRESUMABLY LEAD TO A MORE ORDERLY SOCIETY...

THEY'RE STONING THAT COUPLE TO DEATH FOR **HOLDING HANDS** IN PUBLIC... CARE TO **WATCH**, YOUR HIGHNESS? | NO, THANKS... I'M EAGER TO GET TO MY **ALL-ADOLESCENT BOY HAREM!**

THOUGH IT ALSO WOULD LEAD TO A MORE **UPTIGHT, REPRESSIVE,** AND **HYPOCRITICAL SOCIETY!**

BEHAVIORAL CONTROL SEEMS TO BE DIRECTED PRIMARILY AT WOMEN, THROUGH BOTH LEGAL AND SOCIAL MEANS...

DO I **HAVE** TO WEAR THIS **CHASTITY BELT** UNDER MY PROM DRESS? | **YES!** AND DON'T YOU **DARE** TAKE IT OFF! | **YOUNG MEN** ARE LIKE **SAVAGE BEASTS** ONCE THEY'RE AROUSED, DEAR... | I SHOULD KNOW—**I** WAS YOUNG ONCE **MYSELF,** HA-HA!

THE LOGIC BEHIND THIS IS THAT FEMALES ARE THE GATEKEEPERS (BOTH LITERALLY AND FIGURATIVELY) WHEN IT COMES TO SEXUAL ACTIVITY -- WHILE WE MEN, APPARENTLY, ARE BEYOND ALL HOPE WHEN IT COMES TO SELF-CONTROL.

CITING THE BIBLE (OR THE KORAN) LENDS **MORAL AUTHORITY** TO THESE OUTDATED RULES AND RESTRICTIONS...

"THE MEN SHOUTED, 'BRING OUT YOUR FRIEND SO THAT WE CAN HAVE **ANAL SEX** WITH HIM'... | TO WHICH THE OLD MAN SAID, 'DON'T BE SO **VILE.** HE IS MY **GUEST**'... | '...LOOK, HERE IS MY **VIRGIN DAUGHTER.** YOU MAY DO WITH HER AS YOU **PLEASE,** BUT LEAVE MY GUEST ALONE...'*

?!? WHY DID HE DO **THAT?** | BECAUSE HOMOSEXUALITY IS **DISGUSTING,** DEAR.

* THIS "MORAL" IS TOLD **TWICE** IN THE OLD TESTAMENT!

... EVEN THOUGH THESE ANCIENT TOMES HAPPEN TO BE THE MOST UNABASHEDLY MISOGYNISTIC BOOKS EVER WRITTEN!

"**BE FRUITFUL AND MULTIPLY**" MAY HAVE BEEN SAGE ADVICE BACK WHEN LIFE WAS SHORT AND INFANT MORTALITY HIGH, BUT PROLIFIC PROCREATION IS THE **LAST** THING HUMANITY NEEDS THESE DAYS...

OUR SON JUST BLEW HIMSELF UP IN A **SUICIDE ATTACK!** | TO THE **BEDROOM,** QUICK! | WE MUST MAKE MORE **MARTYRS** RIGHT AWAY! | HURRY, BEFORE THE JEWS **OUTBREED** US!

... UNLESS YOU THINK OF YOUR OWN OFFSPRING AS **CANNON FODDER,** THAT IS -- WHICH PEOPLE **STILL DO** BACK IN THE "HOLY LAND"!

MEANWHILE, BACK IN 21ST-CENTURY AMERICA, OUR PRESIDENT CONTINUES WITH HIS TOTALLY PUNK ROCK "MESSING UP THE SYSTEM FROM WITHIN" STRATEGY BY APPOINTING CONTRACEPTION OPPONENTS IN KEY POSITIONS, SUCH AS:

DR. DAVID HAGER, WHOSE (VERY) MINORITY REPORT TO THE F.D.A. ADVISING AGAINST OVER-THE-COUNTER STATUS FOR PLAN B LED TO IT REMAINING PRESCRIPTION-ONLY FOR **TWO MORE YEARS.**

"GOD TOOK THAT INFORMATION, AND USED IT THROUGH THIS MINORITY REPORT TO INFLUENCE THE DECISION."*

HAGER'S EX-WIFE HAS SINCE TOLD THE PRESS THAT THE GOOD DOCTOR USED TO ROUTINELY **ANALLY RAPE** HER IN HER SLEEP!
*WASHINGTON POST, 5/12/05

DR. ERIC KEROACK, WHO BRIEFLY WAS DEPUTY ASSISTANT DIRECTOR OF "POPULATION AFFAIRS" AT H.H.S. BEFORE QUESTIONS ABOUT MEDICAID FRAUD FORCED HIS RESIGNATION.

"(PREMARITAL SEX) WILL END UP DAMAGING YOUR BRAIN'S ABILITY... TO HELP YOU SUCCESSFULLY **BOND** IN FUTURE RELATIONSHIPS"...*

DUH...

*NY TIMES, 1/26/07

THAT'S RIGHT: HORMONES CAN TELL IF YOU'RE MARRIED! KEROACK ALSO RAN ONE OF THOSE BOGUS "WOMEN'S HEALTH" CLINICS WHOSE SOLE PURPOSE IS TO **DISCOURAGE ABORTIONS.**

KEROACK WAS REPLACED BY DR. SUSAN ORR, WHO OPPOSES GOVERNMENT FUNDING FOR AND PROMOTION OF **CONTRACEPTIVES...**

INCLUDING CONTRACEPTIVES IN GOVERNMENT HEALTH CARE PLANS MAKES US **ALL** COLLABORATORS IN THE **CULTURE OF DEATH**...*

FERTILITY IS **NOT A** DISEASE!**

"REAL WOMEN STAY MARRIED" BY DR. S. ORR***

YET SHE HAS NO PROBLEM SPENDING PUBLIC MONEY ON INEFFECTIVE **ABSTINENCE** PROGRAMS (DISCLOSURE: ORR IS A FORMER DIRECTOR OF SOCIAL POLICY FOR THE REASON FOUNDATION).(*CBS NEWS, 10/19/07, **WASH. POST, 4/12/01, ***WASHINGTON WATCH, 6/00).

AND WHERE DID ALL OF THESE "CONSCIENTIOUS PHARMACISTS" SUDDENLY COME FROM? I CAN'T FIND A SINGLE RECORDED INSTANCE OF A DRUGGIST REFUSING TO FILL A LEGAL PRESCRIPTION FOR A DRUG **OTHER THAN PLAN B!**

AS A DEVOUT CHRISTIAN, I REFUSE TO ASSIST ANYONE IN PERFORMING **ABORTIONS** OR **EUTHANASIA.**

EUTHANASIA? TAKEN IN THE RIGHT (OR WRONG) DOSE, WOULDN'T THAT INCLUDE **MOST** OF WHAT A PHARMACY SELLS?

PLAN B'S CRITICS CLAIM IT WILL ENCOURAGE **PROMISCUITY** AMONG TEENAGERS, THOUGH THERE'S NO EVIDENCE TO BACK UP THIS CLAIM...

I CAN HEAR GRANDPA **GETTIN' BUSY** AGAIN...

IT'S SO **GROSS!**

NO KIDDING...

EVEN MY **IPOD** CAN'T DROWN HIM OUT!

I BLAME IT ON THOSE **PILLS** HE'S TAKING.

UGH!
>UGH!<

MEANWHILE, VIAGRA HAS CONTRIBUTED TO THE SPREAD OF S.T.D.S AMONG THE **ELDERLY,** YET AS FAR AS I KNOW NO PHARMACIST HAS EVER REFUSED TO FILL A PRESCRIPTION FOR **THAT** DRUG!

IT'S HARD NOT TO CONCLUDE THAT PLAIN OL' **RESENTMENT** ALSO IS BEHIND ALL THIS CONTRACEPTIVE HATIN'. AND THESE MISERABLE WRETCHES HAVE **WAY TOO EASY** A TIME MAKING OTHERS FEEL GUILTY...

HMPF... IT SOUNDS LIKE EVERYONE'S **GETTING LAID** TONIGHT EXCEPT FOR **ME** AGAIN...

BUT THIS LETTER TO MY **CONGRESSMAN** WILL HELP PUT A STOP TO THEIR **FUN!**

OOH YEAH...

DO IT, BABY..

WHO'S YER DADDY...

UGH! UGH!

TO THIS I SAY, **DON'T GIVE UP THE FIGHT!** STICK IT TO THE MAN BY FORNICATING YOUR **HEAD OFF!** AND ALWAYS HAVE PLENTY OF PLAN B ON HAND, JUST IN CASE!

Analyze

(1) Some critics call Bagge's work "comic strip essays" because of their heavy reliance on text. Review "The War on Fornication," but read only the text blocks above and below the images—skip over the actual images and the speech bubbles. How effective is this new reading? Does it function well as an essay without the images? How do the images complement the text?

(2) How do the illustrations help you understand and appreciate the author's tone? Given textual examples such as "miserable wretches" and "Stick it to the man by fornicating your head off!" are the illustrations less or more effective than the text itself in communicating tone?

(3) The title of this piece is rendered in a graphic style reminiscent of the posters used to promote 1950s "monster movies." (Feel free to Google "monster movie posters" for numerous examples.) In your opinion, how does this style contribute to the comic's message? Also, why isn't the entire comic presented in this graphic style?

(4) Why is this piece in the "Politics" section? What's political about it? How is the argument in this graphic essay related to social power? What inherent challenges would an author face in asking readers to rethink or change their views on subjects such as sexual expression?

Explore

(1) In a 2013 interview with the *Comics Journal*, Bagge explains, "When I draw women, I just give them the same skinny, loopy, ropy bodies that the males have." Compare his representations of women to those done by other artists in this textbook. What gender-based commentary might Bagge be making with these essentially interchangeable bodies? How is that particularly relevant in an essay like "The War on Fornication"?

(2) Bagge references numerous real-world people near the end of this piece. Dr. David Hager. Dr. Eric Keroack. Dr. Susan Orr. Do a little Google sleuthing on one or more of these people. Does the information you find online match what Bagge presents here? In traditional research papers, students cite their sources in specific ways. How does Bagge attempt to claim a similar level of academic credibility in his argument? Is it effective?

(3) If you were in the position of deciding once and for all whether the government will give out free contraceptives in public schools, what factors would you weigh most heavily before making that choice?

(4) Besides political ads, newspaper articles, editorials, and op-eds, where else do you find people arguing publicly on issues of personal sexual activity? Consider TV shows, websites, magazines, songs, movies, novels, comics, and so on.

The Arts

In some ways, this entire book is about "the arts"—specifically how experience, opinion, and imagination are communicated in word and image. But because this is the first college reader to specifically examine visual narratives, we decided to include a short section on the production of art, specifically as it applies to comics.

To talk about "the arts" is to talk about the act of creation itself. Where do ideas come from? What is the nature of artistic vision? How does a work of art communicate with its audience? For these questions, there is no single answer. Artists express themselves in a variety of ways: they communicate ideas of beauty or desperation through a static image; they press emotional power into a narrative or into a color palette that will define the "feel" of a comic.

But the idea of artistic meaning is difficult to pin down. Does meaning lie with the artist, with the experience or message he or she attempted to convey in the art? Does meaning lie individually with each viewer, so that art becomes what you make of it? Does meaning lie with critics—those people who are specially trained in art or literary history and who might better understand how a work of art contributes to ongoing cultural themes? Does meaning lie with the audience as a whole, with the general consensus culled from many viewers' opinions to the nature of the work? Some might argue that art has no meaning except to nurture the human soul, to create an experience in which the viewer is drawn toward contemplation, reflection, or even something approaching prayer.

The idea of meaning is so difficult (and so important) when it comes to art that for centuries philosophers, artists, and critics have tried to wrestle this experience into language—to offer *unified* understanding of artistic meaning.

> The aim of art is to represent not the outward appearance of things, but their inward significance.
> —Aristotle

> Art is not what you see but what you make others see.
> —Edgar Degas

Art is the desire of a man to express himself, to record the reactions of his
personality to the world he lives in.
—Amy Lowell

Art enables us to find ourselves and lose ourselves at the same time.
—Thomas Merton

Why do so many noteworthy people take the time to understand the nature of art ... and even to defend its importance? Because art—the ability to create work that expresses personal ideas—is central to human experience. Records of visual art extend back 40,000 years: from comic books to canvases, to wood carvings, to pottery, to Indonesian cave paintings made roughly 38,000 years before Christ. This ability to combine personal vision with language or image is uniquely human, an ability of the highest order.

But in an age of science and technology (Mars rovers, iPhones, cars that can drive themselves), some people are asking, does art still have its same value? Does it have relevance—especially when compared to the STEM disciplines? It should come as no surprise that artists take up these questions in art. Or, in our case, in visual essays and visual arguments.

In "Fiction Versus Nonfiction," Chris Ware shows readers how art and memory sometimes capture powerful truths more readily than direct experience. Peter Kuper's *Stop Forgetting to Remember: The Autobiography of Walter Kurtz* shows us a candid look at the daily struggles of being a fortysomething cartoonist, living and working in New York City. Playing off the fiction-versus-nonfiction idea Ware explores, Kuper calls his book an autobiography of Walter Kurtz. Kuper is *not* Kurtz, but who else can write an *auto*biography than the person it's about, right? It's clear that Kurtz's life is greatly informed by Kuper's life, but perhaps again we see that in order to get at crucial understandings, historical truth has to take a small step back—or perhaps to the side—from an imagined truth.

Certainly other pieces in this textbook are, to a greater or lesser extent, an examination of the arts because all art is in some way a commentary on or investigation into art itself. In this section, we ask you to explore with us—to wrestle with large questions: why does art matter, and how, specifically, does it create meaning?

PETER KUPER

Stop Forgetting to Remember: The Autobiography of Walter Kurtz

The prolific Peter Kuper is known to some as the 1979 cofounder of the political comics anthology *World War 3*. To others, he's known for illustrating *Mad* magazine's feature "Spy vs. Spy." And to yet others, he's recognized for artwork that appears regularly in such venues as *Time*, *The New York Times*, *Rolling Stone*, and *The New Yorker*. Since 2006, Kuper has been living in Mexico, where he's been writing about its political situation. *Diario de Oaxaca* is his sketchbook diary chronicling his time there.

The Arts

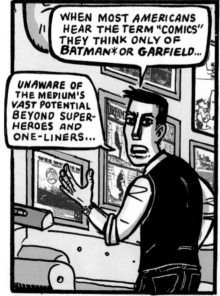

* NOTHING AGAINST BATMAN.

Secrets of the GRAPHIC NOVELIST*

* BOY'S CLUB VERSION

Missing the sports gene...

Recurring rejection and endless ass-kickings...

Enormous (usually unjustified) egotistical belief in one's unrecognized genius...

Repressive, conflicted Judeo-Christian upbringing...

The Arts

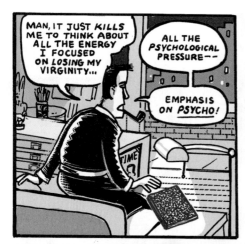

486   The Arts

The Arts

SO THERE I WAS BACK AT SQUARE ONE, STILL HANGING OUT WITH BRAD, STILL A VIRGIN. I HAD TO GIVE BRAD CREDIT THOUGH, HE WAS INVENTIVE WHEN IT CAME TO MEETING THE OPPOSITE SEX, AND ONE OF HIS BETTER IDEAS WAS TO GO DIRECTLY TO AN UNCHALLENGED SOURCE...

THAT CAR'S STOPPING!

WHOOHOO! GIRLS, HERE WE COME!

SCREEEEEE

AN **ALL-GIRLS** CATHOLIC SCHOOL!

Elvis cloud →

I DATED A COUPLE O' CHICKS FROM HERE...

AND LET ME TELL YOU WALT, THEY WERE HOT!

FAR OUT!

IT WAS FUNNY HOW A PLACE THAT PREACHED SUCH A STRICT MORAL CODE REGULARLY PRODUCED GIRLS WHO SMOKED, DRANK, DID MORE DRUGS, AND HAD MORE SEX THAN THEIR PUBLIC SCHOOL COUNTERPARTS!

VERONICA, CAN YOU MEET US IN THE WOODS WITH BETTY?

NEXT PERIOD.

I DON'T WANT TO SEE YOU WITH THOSE DIME STORE EYES AGAIN YOUNG LADY!

BITCH

BOY, THAT IS SOME REALLY GOOD REEFER BETTY!

THANKS.

DO YOU GUYS WANT TO COME OVER TONIGHT?

MY PARENTS ARE OUT OF TOWN!

BEAUTIFUL!

THAT NIGHT WHILE BRAD COMFORTABLY MADE THE MOVES ON BETTY, I UNCOMFORTABLY PLAYED PING-PONG WITH VERONICA...

JEEZ! VERONICA HAS ENORMOUS BREASTS, AND SHE'S NOT WEARING A BRA!

TOUCHÉ!

OH BRAD!

I NEVER NOTICED HOW BLUE YOUR EYES ARE...

The Arts

Analyze

(1) This story starts quietly, without any text or even people (at least none that are featured prominently on the page). How does this type of story beginning affect your reading? What type of connections do you see with this type of beginning and those you find in other graphic narratives? Short stories? Films?

(2) A few panels in, Walter Kurtz turns to you, the reader, and speaks directly. Many stories, plays, and films take a fly-on-the-wall approach, where a reader (or viewer) simply observes the action unfold. Is Kuper doing this because the topic of this story has to do with instruction, or do you think it's a strategy he's employing for different reasons? How does the technique engage you?

(3) In the "Secrets of the Graphic Novelist" section, the color scheme changes to incorporate maroon. Why do you imagine Kuper made that choice? What effect does it have on your reading of the material there? After he shifts back to the black-and-white style, he brings back elements of the new color scheme later to show his diary. How is he using color? Is it relevant that the shade of maroon he chooses could be said to resemble the color of a bruise?

(4) Kurtz claims, "You know art doesn't always have to show things as they are— it can also show the world as we'd like to see it!" What do you make of that claim appearing in an autobiography? And what do you make of an autobiography written about an author's fictional alter ego?

Explore

(1) Early on in this excerpt, Kurtz claims that "art schools have begun offering courses on the subject and a whole new generation of cartoonists are emerging." Is that still true today? Spend a few minutes researching this question to find the answer. And what is the public's—which is to say your own and your classmates'—opinion about the general popularity of cartoons and graphic texts? Is it a form that seems to be declining, holding steady, or expanding?

(2) Why do you think Kuper titled this graphic novel as he did? What connections do you see between the title and issues of identity and memory? What purpose should a title serve? If you had to come up with an alternate title, what would it be? Why?

(3) Visit www.peterkuper.com and read the sections titled "What's New" and "Biography." How does "Stop Forgetting to Remember" fit in with his other work? What connections do you see with what you've discovered about Kuper and his life?

(4) The idea of impending fatherhood has sent Walt down memory lane. What major events in your own life have sent you spiraling down memory lane? Do you have the same level of regret that Walter does? After all, he says "God damn, the fun I could have had if I knew then what I know now!" followed by "@#&$! Youth is wasted on the young!" Do you believe him, or is that just part of a manufactured, performative stance he is using in the comic?

CHRIS WARE

"Fiction Versus Nonfiction"

Chris Ware attended the University of Texas at Austin, where he worked as a cartoonist for the school paper, *The Daily Texan*. Though he began but never finished a master's degree program in printmaking at the Art Institute of Chicago, the graphic elements of printmaking are evident in many of his comics. His work has been featured in *The New Yorker*, *The New York Times*, *Esquire*, and *The Village Voice*, but he is best known for his comic *Jimmy Corrigan: The Smartest Kid on Earth*, a graphic novel that's arguably the most successful book-length comic since Art Spiegelman's *Maus*.

"THE ROLE AUTOBIOGRAPHY PLAYS IN FICTION IS LIKE THAT OF REALITY TO A DREAM. AS YOU DREAM YOUR SHIP, YOU PERHAPS KNOW THE BOAT, BUT YOU'RE GOING TOWARDS A COAST THAT IS QUITE STRANGE, YOU'RE WEARING STRANGE CLOTHES... BUT THE WOMAN ON THE LEFT IS YOUR WIFE."

– JOHN CHEEVER.

FOR YEARS NOW SINCE HER DEATH, I'VE BEEN TRYING TO WRITE ABOUT MY GRANDMOTHER.

EVEN WORSE, I CAN'T BE SURE I'M CORRECTLY RECALLING ANYTHING SHE SAID, THE WORDS CRUMBLING LIKE CLUMPS OF DRY SAND AS I WRITE THEM...

GOOD JOB, SUGARPIE...

OH, IT WON'T KILL YOU...C'MON...

...SHE CROSSED THE DIVIDE BACK INTO THE WORLD OF THE LIVING.

AND FOR CHRIST'S SAKE STOP *BLUBBERING* OR YOU'LL RUIN YOUR SHIRT

:snf:

THE COLLECTIVE MEMORIES OF EVERYTHING SHE EVER WAS TO ME COALESCED AND BLOOMED RIGHT ON THE PAGE...

WHO CARES WHAT THE OTHER KIDS, THINK, ANYWAY?

OKAY, HONEYPIE?

WIFE

...AND AS IN A DREAM, AMIDST MY CONCOCTED POPULACE, SHE KNEW WHAT TO SAY AND HOW TO SAY IT.

SO...WHAT'RE YOU DRAWING?

IT'S BEEN MY ONGOING GOAL TO ATTEMPT A PORTRAIT OF HER BLUNT EBULLIENCE, HER SPIRITED PERSONALITY...

SHE WAS THE MOST WONDERFUL STORYTELLER...

SHE COULD MAKE ANYTHING FUN...DOING LAUNDRY, GROCERY SHOPPING... ⸮sigh⸮...YOU WOULD'VE **LOVED** HER...

BUT EVERY TIME, I FIND MYSELF IMMEDIATELY BOGGED DOWN BY DETAILS, A CREEPING UNCERTAINTY OF MY MEMORY AND OBJECTIVITY...

GRANDMA & ME
A PROFOUNDLY POWERFUL MEMOIR

IT WAS 1975...

NO WAIT... 1976...

GRANDMA, HE'S AFRAID OF GOING TO SCHOOL

PRETEND WORDS

SUGARPLUM SWEETIE PIE

⸮CRY⸮

ONE DAY, HOWEVER, WHILE WORKING ON ONE OF MY "GRAPHIC NOVELS," I AMUSED MYSELF BY DRAWING HER AS A FICTIONAL CHARACTER...

OH, WHAT THE HELL...

...AND SUDDENLY, IN THE SPACE OF ONE OR TWO PANELS...

⸮snf⸮

←PRETEND PEOPLE

UH... A STRIP ABOUT HOW THE FALSENESS OF FICTION FOSTERS AN ENVIRONMENT FOR CERTAIN TRUTHS TO FLOURISH WHILE NON-FICTION KILLS THEM... SORT OF LIKE THE DIFFERENCE BETWEEN ACTING AND IMPERSONATION, OR DRAWING AND ILLUSTRATION... BUT I'M RUNNING OUT OF SPACE TO MORE THOROUGHLY EXPLICATE THOSE METAPHORS, UNFORTUNATELY...

OH

WELL WHO'S THE KID IN GLASSES NEXT TO ME, THEN?

Chris Ware: "Fiction Versus Nonfiction"

Analyze

(1) A comic tier is a line of panels, all of similar height, that move across a page. A daily comic in a newspaper is a perfect comic tier: three or four panels, all of identical height. "Fiction Versus Nonfiction" playfully challenges the way in which we visually move through the comic. The comic layout resists easy tiers. Tall panels are followed by short panels. Panel boxes are presented as a collection of four smaller panels. Discuss your reading experience of this comic. How did you navigate it? How did you create a sequence order for the variously sized panels?

(2) Some comic artists, such as Alison Bechdel, present highly detailed and realistic characters. Ware's characters in this comic, however, appear largely as icons, composed of simple geometric shapes—circles and lines. Yet we recognize them as people. How do you respond to these characters, as compared to more representational figures?

(3) Ware's comics, with their precise lines, simple shapes, and strong organization, are often compared to the graphic work of architects and engineers. "Fiction Versus Nonfiction" is so geometric and flat that it appears to have been produced by a machine. Develop a list of eight words or phrases that describe the visual style of this comic.

(4) In this comic, which makes the characters seem more lifelike: the expressiveness of the drawing or the lines of dialogue they speak?

Explore

(1) "Fiction Versus Nonfiction" suggests that fiction (an artful lie) can offer a reading experience with qualities that differ from nonfiction (the truth). In your opinion, what can fiction convey with more strength than nonfiction?

(2) This comic suggests that human memories are imprecise: people misremember dates, names, and details of important events. If memories are naturally imperfect, what value do you believe they have? What types of experiences— for example, feeling emotions, seeing details, hearing sounds, smelling odors, learning facts, gaining technical skills—are best preserved in human memory?

(3) Perform the following memory test. In class, create a simple line drawing of your bedroom exactly as you left it this morning. Label a dozen items of importance and their location in the room. When you return home later today, compare your drawing with the room. Which items did you correctly describe? Which did you place in the wrong location? Are there items or aspects of the room that you forgot about completely?

(4) Ware uses words and images to retain the memory of his grandmother. First, write a one-page nonfiction description of a day you once spent with a grandparent. Next, write a one-page fictional story in which this same grandparent visits you at college to offer a piece of advice. Which "feels" more real to you: the fiction or the nonfiction?

FURTHER READINGS

For those who want to read more deeply in the field of graphic narratives, the following list is a great place to start. New graphic texts are being created all the time, so let this serve simply as a starting point for your own investigation and exploration into this exciting form of literature.

Identity
- *La Perdida* by Jessica Abel
- *Epileptic* by David B.
- *Marble Season* by Gilbert Hernandez
- *Asterios Polyp* by David Mazzucchelli

Men and Women
- *One! Hundred! Women!* by Lynda Barry
- *Bottomless Belly Button* by Dash Shaw
- *Stitches* by David Small
- *Box Office Poison* by Alex Robinson

Young Adulthood
- *Ghost World* by Daniel Clowes
- *I Never Liked You* by Chester Brown
- *The Wall: Growing Up Behind the Iron Curtain* by Peter Sis
- *Katman* by Kevin C. Pyle
- *Black Hole* by Charles Burns

Trauma
- *Maus* by Art Spiegelman
- *Last Day in Vietnam* by Will Eisner
- *Tricked* by Alex Robinson
- *Safe Area Goražde* by Joe Sacco

History
- *The Beats* by Harvey Pekar
- *The Cartoon History of the Universe III: From the Rise of Arabia to the Renaissance* by Larry Gonick
- *The Great American Dust Bowl* by Don Brown
- *From Hell* by Eddie Campbell and Alan Moore

Politics

- *The Nightly News* by Jonathan Hickman
- *Pyongyang: A Journey in North Korea* by Guy Delisle

The Arts

- *Building Stories* by Chris Ware
- *Cages* by Dave McKean

··

Some Useful Resources About Graphic Narratives

Books

Comics and Sequential Art by Will Eisner
Understanding Comics by Scott McCloud
Reinventing Comics by Scott McCloud
Graphic Novels and Comic Books by Kat Kan

Articles/Essays

Jan Baetens, "From Black & White to Color and Back: What Does It Mean (not) to Use Color?" *College Literature* 38.3 (Summer 2011), 111–128.

Videos

Michael Chaney's TedxDartmouth Talk "How to Read a Graphic Novel"
Jeremy Short's TedxOU Talk "Graphic Textbooks: A Graphic Approach to Higher Education"
Scott McCloud's Ted Talk "The Visual Magic of Comics"

Websites

http://thecomicbookteacher.com/author/rqwhitaker/
http://cbldf.org/
http://www.readingwithpictures.org/
http://noflyingnotights.com/

Preface

p. XIV: Abel, Jessica. "What is a 'Graphic Novel?'" by Jessica Abel, posted at http://dw-wp.com/resources/what-is-a-graphic-novel/. Reprinted by permission of Jessica Abel, http://jessicaabel.com/.

1. Identity

p. 5: Sorese, Jeremy: "Love Me Forever! Oh! Oh! Oh!" by Jeremy Sorese originally appeared in *Little Heart: A Comic Anthology for Marriage Equality*. Reprinted by permission of Jeremy Sorese.

p. 22: Satrapi, Marjane. "The Bicycle," and "The Veil" from *Persepolis: The Story of a Childhood* by Marjane Satrapi, translation copyright © 2003 by L'Association, Paris, France. Used by permission of Pantheon Books, an imprint of the Knopf Doubleday Publishing Group, a division of Penguin Random House LLC. All rights reserved.

p. 39: Glidden, Sarah. Excerpt from *How to Understand Israel in 60 Days or Less* by Sarah Glidden. Copyright 2010 by Sarah Glidden. Reprinted by permission of Sarah Glidden.

p. 52: Corman, Leela. Excerpt from *Unterzakhn* by Leela Corman, copyright © 2012 by Leela Corman. Used by permission of Schocken Books, an imprint of the Knopf Doubleday Publishing Group, a division of Penguin Random House LLC. All rights reserved.

2. Men & Women

p. 69: Davis, Vanessa: "In the Rough," originally published in Tablet Magazine, Dec. 16, 2011. Republished by permission of Vanessa Davis.

p. 74: Drechsler, Debbie. "The Dead of Winter," © Debbie Drechsler 2014. Reprinted by permission of Debbie Drechsler.

p. 82: Bell, Gabrielle. "Cecil and Jordan in New York" from *Cecil and Jordan in New York: Stories* by Gabrielle Bell. Reprinted by permission of *Drawn & Quarterly*.

p. 89: Avril, François and Petit-Roulet, Philippe. "63, rue de la Grange aux Belles" from *Paris Soirees* by François Avril and Philippe Petit-Roulet. © 2012 Humanoids, Inc. Los Angeles. Used by permission.

p. 101: Anderson, Brent. "The Hero" © 2000, 2004 Brent Eric Anderson. Reprinted by permission of Brent Anderson.

p. 113: Cendreda, Martin. "La Brea Woman" by Martin Cendreda, appeared in *Mome*, Spring/Summer 2006. Reprinted by permission of Martin Cendreda.

p. 121: Huizenga, Kevin: "Glenn Ganges in Pulverize" from *Ganges #2* by Kevin Huizenga. Used by permission of Kevin Huizenga.

3. Young Adulthood

p. 146: Bechdel, Alison. "Old Father, Old Artificer" from *Fun Home: A Family Tragicomic* by Alison Bechdel. Copyright © 2006 by Alison Bechdel. Reprinted by permission of Houghton Mifflin Harcourt Publishing Company. All rights reserved.

p. 169: Bell, Gabrielle. "Amy was a Babysitter" from *When I'm Old and Other Stories* by Gabrielle Bell. Copyright © Gabrielle Bell. Reprinted by permission of Gabrielle Bell.

p. 174: Barry, Lynda. "San Francisco" by Lynda Barry from *One Hundred Demons* (Sasquatch Books, 2002). Copyright © 2002 by Lynda Barry. Used with permission. All rights reserved.

p. 181: Bell, Gabrielle. "When I was Eleven" from *Lucky* by Gabrielle Bell. Reprinted by permission of *Drawn & Quarterly*.

p. 188: Derf Backderf. "The Bank" from *Punk Rock & Trailer Parks* by Derf. Reprinted by permission of Derf.

p. 212: Mutch, Kevin. "Blue Note" from *Fantastic Life* by Kevin Mutch, copyright 2010 by Kevin Mutch. Lyrics from "The Advocate" © 1983 written by Mitch Funk and Jimmy Green of Personality Crisis. Reprinted by permission. All rights reserved.

p. 230: Bennett, Jonathan: "Dance with the Ventures," copyright © 2015, Jonathan Bennett. Reprinted by permission of Jonathan Bennett.

4. Trauma

p. 247: Brooks, Max and Caanan White. Excerpt(s) from *The Harlem Hellfighters* by Max Brooks, illustrated by Caanan White, copyright © 2014 by Max Brooks. Used by permission of Broadway Books, an imprint of the Crown Publishing Group, a division of Random House LLC. All rights reserved.

p. 272: Sacco, Joe. "Complacency Kills" from the book *Journalism* by Joe Sacco. Copyright © 2012 by Joe Sacco. Used by permission of Henry Holt and Company, LLC. All rights reserved.

p. 282: Gipi. From *Notes for a War Story* © 2007 by Gipi. Reprinted by permission of First Second, an imprint of Roaring Brook Press, a division of Holtzbrinck Publishing Holdings Limited Partnership. All rights reserved.

p. 305: Ames, Jonathan and Haspiel, Dean. From *The Alcoholic* by Jonathan Ames, illustrated by Dean Haspiel. Reprinted by permission of William Morris Endeavor Entertainment.

Anderson, Brent. "The Hero" © 2000, 2004 Brent Eric Anderson. Reprinted by permission of Brent Anderson.

5. History

6. Politics

7. The Arts

p. 471: Kuper, Peter. From *Stop Forgetting to Remember (The Autobiography of Walter Kurtz)* by Peter Kuper. Copyright © 2007 Peter Kuper. Reprinted by permission of Peter Kuper.

p. 497: Ware, Chris. "Fiction Versus Nonfiction" was first published in ArtForum. © Chris Ware 2015. Reprinted by permission of Chris Ware and Aragi Inc.